Historical Films in the Latin Classroom

Jeffrey L. Buller

The American Classical League
Miami University
Oxford, Ohio 45056

This publication is available from
The American Classical League
Miami University, Oxford, Ohio 45056
www.aclclassics.org

Copyright 1992
By The American Classical League

ISBN 0-939507-39-0

Historical Films in the Latin Classroom

The extraordinary popularity of the videocassette recorder in recent years has given the Latin teacher access to an unprecedented amount of audiovisual material.[1] The declining cost of buying prerecorded videotapes -- and it is now frequently possible to purchase a movie for far less than the cost to rent it only a few years ago -- has meant that schools all across the country have assembled vast libraries of motion pictures. One advantage of such a collection cannot be denied: after a videotape has been purchased, it is available whenever it is needed; it may be used as often as the teacher wishes and does not have to be ordered far in advance from a distant film library.

But the Latin teacher who is attracted by that advantage is likely to be disappointed. For the vast majority of videotapes now available are "feature entertainments," films which were intended to please rather than to inform. As a result, we may wonder: is there any educational value to be found in a work of this sort? And, even if there is, how might the film be best co-ordinated with other, more traditional material? In fact, is it even legal for teachers to use a pre-recorded videotape, usually distributed "for home use only," within the very public setting of the Latin classroom? These are important questions, and they raise issues which must be addressed if classicists are to use the new technology effectively. So it seems best to deal with each of these topics individually, beginning perhaps with the last.

The Legality of Using Historical Films in the Latin Class

> **WARNING:** This motion picture has been licensed for *private exhibition* and *home viewing* only, without charge of any kind. Any other use of this cassette, including any *performance in public*, copying, or reproduction of any portion thereof is an infringment of copyright and may result in civil liability and severe criminal penalties as provided by law. The Federal Bureau of Investigation examines allegations of copyright infringement. [Title 17 USC, Sections 501, 506.]

Anyone who has ever rented a movie will recognize this warning at once. It appears on the label of nearly every videocassette sold or rented in America. Unfortunately, the warning's restriction against "any performance in public" causes many teachers to feel uneasy about using videotapes in their courses. What, after all, could be more "public" than viewing a film in a classroom with perhaps twenty or thirty students?

---

[1] This article originally appeared in *The Classical Outlook* 69.1 (Fall 1991) 3-7.

These misgivings may be common, but they are also unfounded. Sections 102 and 110 of the so-called "new copyright law" [i.e., Public Law 94-553 which has been in effect now since January 1, 1978], as well as a major report filed later by the Judiciary Committee of the House of Representatives [U.S. Congress, House, Judiciary Committee, Report No. 94-1476], specifically state that most academic use of videotapes is permissable. (One comprehensive survey of this issue is Miller, 1988). The showing of copyrighted material in a classroom falls within the "fair use" provisions of the copyright law as long as it adheres to the following three guidelines:

1. The videotape must be shown for a genuine educational purpose and that purpose must be directly related to the regular material of the course. (Section 110[2][a-b], reiterated in House Report 94-1476) *Thus viewing a film merely for entertainment or as a reward at the end of the semester would be prohibited.*

2. The videotape must be shown in the classroom itself or at least in a similar academic setting. (Section 110[2][i]) *Thus showing a videotape in an open room at a public library or at another facility similarly used by the public at large would be prohibited.*

3. The videotape must be shown without any fee, and neither the teacher nor the school must secure a profit or obtain a commercial advantage of any kind. (Section 110[4]) *Thus charging the students for admission or using the film to raise funds for an extracurricular activity would be prohibited.*

The first and third of these guidelines are quite easy to follow. To comply with the first restriction, the teacher must simply indicate the cultural or historical information which the students are expected to gain from the film. The third restriction requires even less; students rarely, if ever, need to be told that a classroom film is being shown without charge!

But that second rule, with its limitation that the videotape be shown "in the classroom itself or in a similar academic setting," may cause some confusion. For instance, does the law allow several classes to view the film at the same time in an auditorium, school library or multi-purpose room? Could some other type of facility be used if the film must be shown outside of school hours? In each of these cases the answer is usually "yes." The copyright law permits students to view a videocassette anywhere and at any time, provided only that the facility (1) is not open to the public at large and (2) may be regarded as a "classroom" while the film is actually being shown. (See Reed 35-36 and also her contribution in Galvin and Mason 113-114. Talab 41 notes that a "suitable academic setting" *may* even "include a library, gym, auditorium, or workshop, provided it is used as a class-

room." Strong 135 goes further and suggests that viewing may take place anywhere "on campus or, if off campus, in classroom-type circumstances and classroom-type surroundings.")

Now, it should be noted that all of these guidelines apply only to videotapes which have been *purchased* or *rented* either by the teacher or by the school itself. The guidelines specifically do *not* apply to material which has been taped during a television broadcast. In this case, special restrictions apply and teachers are urged to be extremely careful. For example, one important restriction is that copyrighted material may not be recorded "off the air" for classroom use *at all* if the program is currently available for purchase, rental or broadcast by subscription television (see Talab 37 and Sinofsky 98-102). Since all of the films which will be discussed in this article fall into one or more of these categories, none of them may be legally recorded for classroom use from broadcast or cable television. (For a complete discussion of "off-air" taping and the guidelines of the House Subcommittee on Courts, Civil Liberties, and Administration of Justice, see: Sinofsky 78-88, 98-102, 121-125; Talab 37-41, 124-125; Reed 39-43; and AECT 10). The remarks which follow, therefore, are written upon the assumption that the teacher has rented or purchased an authorized copy of the film.

Using Historical Films as Sources of Cultural Information

One of the most common uses of historical films in Latin courses today is as sources of cultural or factual information about ancient Rome. Many teachers use movies as little more than supplements to the textbook or as an enjoyable way of reviewing material. This type of exercise is certainly valuable but, if carried no further, it fails to take full advantage of everything that historical films have to offer.

As Tom Carr has noted (see Carr, 1989), there are really four different types of information provided by each historical film:

1. **Historical events:** Incidents which occur or are mentioned in the film may be used to review the history of a period.
2. **Historical personages:** Characters appearing in the film are frequently based upon figures familiar to the students and thus may be used to promote discussion about the lives or personalities of these individuals.
3. **Physical setting:** "Buildings, furniture, clothes, food, and the like" must be recreated for the film and thus can expose the student

to an important aspect of daily life in ancient Rome (compare Carr 85).

4. **Social roles, institutions and value systems of an age:** These may be explored as students observe how various characters in the film interact with one another.

Carr (84-86) provides a complete discussion of how classes may analyze factual information in historical films.

Movies can do far more than teach history. They can *show* a class the costumes, customs and warfare of the ancient Greeks and Romans far better than an ordinary textbook can. Approached in this way, historical films perform many of the same functions found in historical novels (see Buller, 1989): they can be used along with more traditional sources of information (classroom texts, historical summaries, classical handbooks, and the like) to bring an entire period of history to life for a class. The film's ability to show students what it was like to *live* in Periclean Athens or Republican Rome -- giving each viewer a sense that he or she is actually there -- represents a significant part of the film's appeal to the Latin teacher.

So important, in fact, is this appeal of historical films that many teachers may wish to adopt a "four year cycle" of movies for their classes. Under this system, one film would be shown each year whenever the appropriate material is encountered during the regular semester. For instance, *Spartacus* might be shown to first year Latin students when they are covering the material on gladiators or Roman slavery commonly found in introductory textbooks; *Cleopatra* might be shown to second year students as part of the unit on Julius Caesar; *Ben-Hur* might be shown in the third year Latin course to supplement the material found in Cicero's texts on such subjects as Roman warfare (*Pro Lege Manilia*), Roman government (*In Lucium Catilinam*) or tensions in the Roman provinces (*In Gaium Verrem*); and *A Funny Thing Happened On The Way To The Forum* might be shown in the fourth year Latin course as a way of exploring the nature of Roman comedy during a special unit on Plautus and Terence.

The schedule on which these films are shown will affect the type of exercises which the students are assigned. For example, if the film *Ben-Hur* were to be shown to more advanced Latin students as part of a unit on Roman warfare, the class might be given a study guide which contains focus questions such as these:

1. How is the pace of the rowers maintained in the Roman galley which we see?
2. How many rowers are assigned to this Roman galley? How many of these rowers are relieved every hour?

3. Which weapons are used by the Romans during the naval battle itself?

Each of these questions is written in such a way that it can be answered in a few words or with a brief phrase. Requiring the students to write long answers while a film is in progress will only distract them, causing them to miss important information and possibly lose track of the plot altogether. Once the movie is over, however, short questions provide the teacher with a convenient opportunity to begin more extensive discussions of naval warfare. While the movie is still fresh in the students' minds, the teacher might ask: "What seems to have been the most important naval strategy used by the Romans in the battle which we saw? How did the Romans attempt to sink or capture the enemy ships? Can you recall any of the actual naval battles that were mentioned in our reading this semester?"

To reinforce these points, individual students might then be assigned oral reports on such topics as the trireme, the quinquereme, the *corvus*, *naumachiae*, the Battle of Corycus [Livy 36.44], C. Duilius and the Battle of Mylae, M. Vipsanius Agrippa, the Battle of Actium, the Battle of Naulochus, and so on. These reports help students to benefit, not only from the material which they present themselves, but also from what they hear in the reports of others.

As a further refinement, the teacher might even use the day of each report as a time to discuss relevant passages of ancient authors, such as Tacitus' description of the naumachia held during the reign of Claudius (*Ann.* 12.56-57), Vergil's (*Aen.* 8.675-731] or Horace's (*Carm.* 1.37 and *Epod.* 1.9) references to the Battle of Actium, or even Thucydides' famous statement on the importance of naval power (1.4-19). The teacher may also wish to contrast Alfred Thayer Mahan's famous view on the vital role of the navy in achieving military supremacy, presented in his *The Influence of Sea Power* books (1893, 1918), to Chester G. Starr's recent rejection of that view, in *The Influence of Sea Power on Ancient History* . The Latin passages, at least, may be read in the original, providing a direct link between the film and the material of the course. In either case, the film -- now complemented by texts, discussions and reports -- will be given a dimension which it could not have achieved on its own.

Correcting the Errors in Historical Films

On certain occasions, a film may be used to reinforce the facts about a period even when the film itself is in error or is misleading (see Buller, 1990, 114). For instance, the movie *Alexander the Great* leaves the strong impression that Roxane was Darius' daughter; the teacher who takes a moment to mention Roxane's actual ancestry will not only be able

to correct this false impression but will also have a convenient opportunity to review the lineage of Darius and Alexander themselves. In a similar way, to compensate for the fictional elements appearing in the film *Spartacus*, a teacher might assign the class those sections from Plutarch's *Life of Crassus* (8-11) which deal with the revolt of the gladiators. Then, comparing what they have seen in the film to what they have read in Plutarch, students might be asked such questions as these: "After they escape from their training camp, in which direction do Spartacus and the other gladiators head in Plutarch's account? How does this differ from the direction in which the slaves are heading in the film?" or "How, according to Plutarch, did Spartacus die? How did Spartacus die in the movie? Why, do you suppose, the author of the screenplay changed this part of the plot when creating the movie?" The last question, in particular, allows the teacher to discuss the use of "creative license" by the authors of historical films and novels. Plutarch, too, as we learn in the introduction to his *Life of Alexander*, never intended to describe events with complete precision, preferring to write an interpretive biography rather than a literal history; from this perspective, at least, our ancient sources bear some resemblance to modern film.

Moreover, as Tom Carr has noted (see Carr 86-89), it can be useful for a class to identify the clichés or stereotypes about the past which appear in an historical film. Frequently, historical films contain, not so much an accurate portrayal of past societies, as a later age's impressions, interpretations or reappraisals of those societies. Greece and Rome, in particular, have been idealized by the modern world and thus their images on film have been strongly influenced by the symbolic value which the classical age has come to assume. By recognizing the presence of this distortion, students will be encouraged to separate the real from the fictitious elements in a film; they will also come to understand how their own expectations may affect their views of the past. Why, for instance, in a film such as *Alexander the Great*, do the vast majority of the soldiers lack scars or any other injuries from battle? Why do the temples and other buildings appear so starkly white even though we know that they were brightly painted in antiquity? Why do the towns contain so many open spaces although many of them must actually have been cramped and crowded? Consideration of these and similar issues will enable a class to discuss both what is known about antiquity and what the modern world has come to *believe* about the ancient world. Students will re-evaluate their own perceptions and stereotypes even while they are developing a more accurate view of the ancient world.

Even in cases where a movie is not really in error, the teacher may use the *partial* presentation of the truth to lead the students towards a more complete understanding of what actually occurred. For example, a class which has just seen the movie *Ben-Hur* might be given an assignment such as this: "In the film, we saw that golden dolphins were used

to count the laps of the race. See if you can find out what *other* devices were used, especially in the Circus Maximus, to count these laps." The reference to the Circus Maximus in this assignment will suggest to the students how they might research the topic. The question will also enable the teacher to shift the discussion gradually away from the film itself to the larger issue of Roman charioteers and the *ludi circenses*. Since the introductory volumes of many textbook series contain information on these very topics, the movie will provide a convenient opportunity for the class to begin exploring the information found there.

Using Historical Films to "Frame" a Discussion or Lesson

While historical films may add an important dimension to the Latin class, they do have one practical disadvantage: their length. *Alexander the Great* is more than two hours long, *Ben-Hur* is three and a half, and *Cleopatra* runs to just over four hours. Even a much shorter film such as *A Funny Thing Happened On The Way To The Forum* cannot be viewed during a single class period. The result all too often is that the movie must be shown a piece at a time over several days or even weeks. Students find it exceedingly difficult to follow the plot of a film which is parceled out in this way: minor characters become confusing to them; the details which the teacher had hoped to review with the film become lost in the shuffle.

Nevertheless, it is possible to make a virtue of necessity, using brief portions of an historical film to their best advantage. This is done by showing a few minutes of an historical film to introduce the class period itself. The movie "sets the mood" for the Latin class; it captures the students' attention and focus it upon the material which they are about to cover. Showing a scene or two each day from a movie such as *Cleopatra*, for instance, will provide a convenient introduction to the day's reading from Caesar at the same time that the film clarifies Caesar's references to legionary standards, "the turtle" (i.e., the *testudo* or tortoise formation), the *pilum* and the *ballista*.

When an historical film is used in this way, the teacher should begin showing the movie almost immediately after the class has begun to study a new author or text. After all, students will have a better understanding of objects used in Roman life if they have observed their use *before* encountering the words for these objects in literature. The film will serve as a visual reinforcement to the text, enabling the student immediately to comprehend references which an author has made.

A more practical reason for showing historical films early in a new unit is that this is usually when time is available for this type of project. Students who are unfamiliar with

the vocabulary and style of a new author often find their first few lessons in a work to be particularly challenging. As a result, the amount of Latin which a class can reasonably master each day at the start of a new text may be relatively short; less than a full class period may be needed to translate and discuss it. In the time which remains, the teacher may wish to review a few principles of grammar, to present new material about Roman art or society, to conduct a vocabulary drill or oral exercise . . . or to show an historical film.

A few minutes of a movie may even be shown while the teacher is taking attendance or returning papers; this will help the students to set aside what they were doing in the last class and to begin thinking about ancient Rome. Then, it may be possible for another brief segment of the film to be shown at the *end* of the class; this will serve as a reward for the students at a time when they are likely to find the text itself particularly difficult. It is especially important to provide this type of reward in second year Latin courses when students are often making a critical decision as to whether they will continue with Latin. The extra appeal provided by historical films can help retain student interest and develop a class' enthusiasm towards their studies.

In certain cases, this division of a film into segments for both the beginning and the end of a class period will result in too much fragmentation. In these situations, it is better to save the entire day's viewing for a block of fifteen or twenty minutes at the end of the hour. With this arrangement, students will quickly realize that the more accurately and thoroughly they prepare their assignments, the more time they will have available to view the film. The film thus provides the students with an added inducement to prepare their translations and other work carefully.

Using Historical Films in Conjunction with Special Projects or Events

There is also one other advantage to showing an historical film shortly after beginning a new unit or text: it may provide the class with ideas for special projects or papers. Seeing the chariot race in *Ben-Hur*, for example, or the arrangement of Crassus' troops in *Spartacus* may inspire a student to conduct additional research on this topic. Other students may decide to investigate Roman dress, architecture or cooking. If the teacher has prepared bibliographies on these topics or, better yet, has the actual books on hand, discussions of a film may be used to transform the students' initial enthusiasm towards the film itself into an early start on a semester long project.

Moreover, since the videotape of an historical film is usually owned by the teacher or by the school as a whole, it can be made available to the students throughout the semester as their work on these projects continues. Thus, the student who decides to make

a Roman costume, prepare a Roman meal, or build a model of a Roman ship can refer to the film whenever necessary. For certain topics, it may even be helpful to begin a report by showing the class a brief portion of a film which they have already seen. The class will thus be able to review familiar information and to visualize what they are about to hear in the student's report.

In certain courses, it may even be possible to use one film to suggest topics for the reports and another film to promote discussion when it is time for the reports to be presented. For instance, both *Ben-Hur* and *Masada* deal with the issue of conflict between the Romans and the Jews in the province of Judaea; this topic may thus be introduced by having the students watch one film and concluded by the reading of papers which have been co-ordinated with the second film. More ambitiously, in a second year Latin course, the teacher might show the film *Spartacus* early in the year when students have successfully completed their review of Latin vocabulary and grammar. In the resulting discussions about the history and culture of the late Republic, the teacher might begin assigning more extensive semester projects: one student might be given the topic of Roman slavery, another might research slave rebellions, a third might be interested in the social status of gladiators, and so on. Then, later in the semester, these projects could be included in a larger unit about Roman slavery and the relationship between masters and slaves in ancient Rome. To renew the class' interest in this topic, the teacher might show a film such as *A Funny Thing Happened On The Way To The Forum* which contains a humorous view of Roman masters and slaves. If the course schedule permits, the film and the reports might even begin on December 17, the first day of the Saturnalia, a holiday on which the Roman distinctions between master and slave were traditionally relaxed.

Indeed, with a little bit of research and creativity it is almost always possible to select some appropriate day for the showing of an historical film. Agnes Michels' useful series "Roman Festivals" (see Michels 1990 and 1991) and Van L. Johnson's *The Roman Origins of Our Calendar* (see Johnson 1958, 1969, 1974, available as item B406 through the American Classical League's Teaching Materials and Resource Center) both contain information on important events and holidays throughout the year. By selecting a proper occasion for the film and by mentioning this to the class, the teacher will give the resulting discussions an added dimension and relate them more easily to the other material of the course. Thus, for instance, *Ben-Hur* might be viewed on one of the days during the Roman year which were traditionally reserved for major games and circuses; these include January 13 (the *Iovi statori circenses*), April 19 (the *Cerealia* and *ludi circenses*), May 12 (the *ludi Marti in circo*) or September 4 (the *ludi Romani*). The film *Fall of the Roman Empire* might be shown on April 26, which was the birthday of Marcus Aurelius. *Cleopatra* might be

shown on the Ides of March or on September 2 (the date of the Battle of Actium). In a course where the achievements of Alexander the Great are being compared to those of Julius Caesar, the film *Alexander the Great* might be shown on March 27 (the date on which Caesar recovered Alexandria) or even, in a summer session, on July 12 (Caesar's birthday).

Another convenient occasion for the showing of historical films is during Foreign Language Week or on a local Latin Day. Once again, by co-ordinating the film with student reports, projects, and other special events, the teacher can reinforce the relationship between the movie and the more traditional material of the course. Moreover, this type of school event enables the Latin teacher to reach out to other potential students and to demonstrate to them that a Latin class consists of more than just declensions and vocabulary drills. For this reason, the teacher might consider opening the event to several other classes: a media class, for instance, might discuss the production and artistry of a film; an English class might discuss its symbolism; and the Latin class could provide the other students with background information and explain the inscriptions, customs and allusions which appear in the film itself. In this way, each group of students would be able to learn from the other, causing the value of the exercise to increase proportionately.

* * *

No matter how historical films are to be used in the Latin class, however, and no matter which films are chosen, it is important for the teacher always to prepare carefully before viewing the film with a class. It cannot be said forcefully enough: previewing is *essential*. Community standards differ, after all, and a film which is perfectly acceptable for use in one school district may not be appropriate elsewhere. In addition, previewing the film will allow the teacher to prepare a few introductory comments on characters, background or setting which will help the students to appreciate what they are about to see. Finally, thorough preparation may enable the teacher to begin relating the film to the other material of the course days, or even weeks, before the film is actually shown. By taking all of these steps, therefore, the teacher will guarantee that the exercise is both enjoyable to the students and an important contribution to their knowledge of the classical world.

Films Mentioned In This Article

Alexander the Great. [Richard Burton]. Copyright 1955 Rossen Films, S.A. Copyright renewed 1983 United Artists Corporation. Distributed on videocassette by MGM/UA Home Video, 1350 Avenue of the Americas, New York, NY, 10019.

Ben-Hur. [Charlton Heston]. Copyright 1959 Loew's Incorporated. Copyright renewed 1987 Turner Entertainment Co. Distributed on videocassette by MGM/UA Home Video Inc., 1000 Washington Boulevard, Culver City, CA, 90232.

Cleopatra. [Elizabeth Taylor]. Copyright 1963 Twentieth Century-Fox Productions, Ltd. Distributed on videocassette by CBS/Fox Video, 39000 Seven Mile Road, Livonia, MI, 48152.

The Fall of the Roman Empire. [Sophia Loren]. Copyright 1961 Samuel Bronston Productions Inc. Distributed on videocassette by United Entertainment Inc., 6535 East Skelly Drive, Tulsa, OK, 74145.

A Funny Thing Happened On The Way To The Forum. [Zero Mostel]. Copyright 1966 Quadrangle Films and United Artists Corporation. Distributed on videocassette by Twentieth Century-Fox Video, Industrial Park Drive, Farmington Hills, MI, 48024. Masada. [Peter O'Toole]. Copyright 1980 by Universal City Studios Inc. Distributed on videocassette by MCA Home Video, 70 Universal City Plaza, Universal City, CA, 91608.

Spartacus. [Kirk Douglas]. Copyright 1960 Universal International and Bryna Productions. Distributed on videocassette by MCA Home Video, 70 Universal City Plaza, Universal City, CA, 91608.

References

Association for Educational Communications and Technology [AECT]. *Copyright and Educational Media*. Washington, DC: Association of Media Producers, 1977.

Buller, Jeffrey L., "Historical Novels in the Latin Classroom." *CO* 66 (1989) 73-77.

_____, "The Roman Empire from Cradle to Graves: Using I, Claudius in the Latin Language or Roman Civilization Course" in *Realizing the Potential of Foreign Language Instruction*, 1990 Report of the Central States Conference on the Teaching of Foreign Languages, edited by Gerard L. Ervin. Lincolnwood, IL: National Textbook Company, 1990. Pages 112-122.

Carr, Tom. "The Past Meets the Present: A Guide to Historical Feature Films in the French Culture Class" in *Defining the Essentials for the Foreign Language Classroom*, 1989 Report of the Central States Conference on the Teaching of Foreign Languages, edited by Dave McAlpine. Lincolnwood, IL: National Textbook Company, 1989. Pages 82-92.

Galvin, Thomas J., and Mason, Sally. "Video, Libraries and the Law: Finding the Balance," *American Libraries* 20.2 (February 1989) 110-119.

Johnson, Van L. *The Roman Origins of Our Calendar*. Oxford, OH: American Classical League, 1958, 1969, 1974.

Mahan, Alfred Thayer. *The Influence of Sea Power Upon the French Revolution and Empire, 1793-1812*. London, ENG: Sampson Low, Marston Co., 1893

_____, *The Influence of Sea Power Upon History, 1660-1783*. Boston, MA: Little, Brown and Co., 1918.

Michels, Agnes K., "Roman Festivals: April-June," *CO* 67 (90) 70-71; "July-September," *CO* 67 (90) 114-116; "October-December," *CO* 68 (91) 10-12; "January-March," *CO* 68 (91) 44-48.

Miller, Jerome K. *Using Copyrighted Videocassettes in Classrooms, Libraries and Training Centers*, second edition. Washington, DC: Copyright Information Service, 1988.

Reed, Mary Hutchings. *The Copyright Primer for Librarians and Educators*. Washington, DC: American Library Association/ National Education Association, 1987.

Sinofsky, E. *Off-Air Videotaping in Education: Copyright Issues, Decision, Implications*. New York, NY: R.R. Bowker, 1984.

Starr, Chester G. *The Influence of Sea Power on Ancient History*. New York, NY: Oxford University Press, 1988.

Strong, William S. *The Copyright Book: A Practical Guide*, second edition. Cambridge, MA: MIT Press, 1981, 1984.

Talab, R.S. *Commonsense Copyright: A Guide to the New Technologies*. Jefferson, NC: McFarland and Company, 1986.

Appendices

A. Select Bibliography on the Use of Feature Films in the Classroom

Amelio, Ralph. *Film in the Classroom*. Dayton, OH: Pflaum Publishing, 1971.

Bryan, Margaret B. and Davis, Boyd H. *Writing About Literature and Film*. New York, NY: Harcourt Brace Jovanovich, 1975.

Carr, Tom. "The Past Meets the Present: A Guide to Historical Feature Films in the French Culture Class" in *Defining the Essentials for the Foreign Language Classroom*, edited by Dave McAlpine. Lincolnwood, IL: National Textbook Company, 1989.

Carr, Tom and Duncan, Jan. "The VCR Revolution: Feature Films for Language and Cultural Proficiency" in *Proficiency, Policy, and Professionalism in Foreign Language Education*, edited by Diane W. Birckbichler. Lincolnwood, IL: National Textbook Company, 1987.

Foster, H.M. *The New Literacy: The Language of Film and Television*. Urbana, IL: National Council of Teachers of English, 1979.

Howe, Michael J.A. *Learning from Television: Psychological and Educational Research*. New York, NY: Harcourt Brace Jovanovich, 1983.

Martin, C.E. and Stainbrook, G.L. "An Analysis Checklist for Audiovisuals When Used as Educational Resources," *Health Education* 17 (August/September 86) 31-33.

Maynard, Richard A. *Classroom Cinema*. New York, NY: Teachers College Press, 1977.

Miller, Hannah Elsas. *Films in the Classroom: A Practical Guide*. Metuchen, NJ: The Scarecrow Press, 1979.

Smith, Paul, editor. *The Historian and Film*. Cambridge: Cambridge University Press, 1976

Sorlin, Pierre. *The Film in History: Restaging the Past*. Totowa, NJ: Barnes and Noble, 1980.

B. Checklist for "Fair Use" of Copyrighted Videotapes in Schools

1. *The videotape must be shown for a genuine educational purpose and that purpose must be directly related to the regular material of the course.* (Section 110[2][a-b], reiterated in House Report 94-1476) Thus viewing a film merely for entertainment or as a reward at the end of the semester would be prohibited.
2. *The videotape must be shown in the classroom itself or in a similar academic setting.* (Section 110[2][i]) Thus showing a videotape in an open room at a public library or at another facility similarly used by the public at large would be prohibited.
3. *The videotape must be shown without any fee, and neither the teacher nor the school must secure a profit or obtain a commercial advantage of any kind.* (Section 110[4]) Thus charging the students for admission or using the film to raise funds for an extracurricular activity would be prohibited.

C. Checklist of Necessary Materials for A Unit on an Historical Film

1] VHS videotape of the film [purchase or rental]
2] VHS videocassette recorder [1/2"]
3] television monitor
4] student copies of the study guide
5] student copies of the co-ordinated texts
6] student copies of the recommended topics for research projects
7] student copies of the quiz
8] student copies of the examination
9] [extension cords? carts? three-way adapter plugs?]

On the following pages, you will find study units designed for use with several historical films commonly shown in Latin courses. Each of these study units includes the following materials:

LESSON PLANS
unit topic
unit objectives
teacher activities
student activities
DISCUSSION TOPICS FOR CO-ORDINATED TEXTS
RESEARCH TOPICS
STUDY GUIDE
SAMPLE QUIZ AND EXAMINATION QUESTIONS

Alexander the Great

UNIT TOPIC
Generals as Statesmen: A Unit on the Film *Alexander the Great*

UNIT OBJECTIVES
Students of second year Latin, after reading Julius Caesar's Gallic Wars, will use the 1955 film *Alexander the Great* to:
- a] compare and contrast the careers and personalities of Alexander the Great and Julius Caesar
- b] examine similarities between the end of the Classical Period in Greece and the fall of the Roman Republic in Italy
- c] discuss the important role which individuals may play in shaping world events

TEACHER ACTIVITIES
1] Before the film:
   - --briefly summarize the major events occurring in Greece during the fourth century B.C. and the outcome of Philip II's early campaigns
   - --locate on a map: Macedon, Persia, Pella, Chaeronea, the Granicus River, Issus, Susa
   - --identify Aristotle, Demosthenes and Aeschines
   - --as an historical reference, remind the students what is occurring in Rome and Italy at this time [the Samnite Wars, the Latin War]
2] After the film is over, review with the students what the movie has taught them movie about:
   - --education in Greece and Macedon
   - --ancient warfare
   - --the extent of the Macedonian Empire at the end of the Classical Period
3] Assign research projects related to the issues raised in the film
4] Translate with the class and discuss the co-ordinated texts [Aulus Gellius *Noctes Atticae* 5.2 and Suetonius *The Life of the Deified Julius* 61]
5] Have the students consider the "additional discussion questions" which appear at the end of the study guide
6] Provide a quiz on the film and co-ordinated readings; discuss the quiz; provide an examination reinforcing the same material
7] Correct and return to each student the study guide, quiz, examination and research project

STUDENT ACTIVITIES
1] Watch the film *Alexander the Great*
2] Complete, fully and correctly, the assigned study guide
3] Participate in all class discussions
4] Translate the co-ordinated texts [Aulus Gellius *Noctes Atticae* 5.2 and Suetonius *The Life of the Deified Julius* 61]
5] Attain a minimum grade of 80 on the quiz
6] Attain a minimum grade of 80 on the examination
7] Complete one of the assigned research projects for a final grade

DISCUSSION TOPICS [FOR CO-ORDINATED TEXTS]

1] Aulus Gellius *Noctes Atticae* 5.2
- --what was the name of Alexander's horse? why was it given this name?
- --from what you know about Roman coinage, does the price of this horse seem to have been high?
- --what did Aulus Gellius consider to be a "memorable" [*dignum memoria*] characteristic of this horse?
- --what noble act did this horse perform during Alexander's campaign in India?
- --what did the horse do "with a sense of relief that was almost human" [*quasi cum sensus humani solacio*]?
- --which city in India was named after this horse?

2] Suetonius *The Life of the Deified Julius* 61
- --which unusual physical characteristic was Caesar's horse said to have had?
- --where did the horse come from?
- --what did the soothsayers [*haruspices*] say about this horse?
- --what is the most obvious similarity between Caesar's horse and that of Alexander?
- --where did Caesar place a statue of this horse? [do you know where this temple was located?]

3] Answer the following questions after you have read both passages:
- --why might biographers have been so eager to say that important generals such as Alexander or Caesar rode "special horses"? [what similar possession might we like to attribute to a hero or leader today?]
- --which details make these two horses "almost human" in the two stories? why might it be important for an heroic figure to ride a horse distinguished in such a way?
- --what are some *other* ways in which Alexander the Great and Julius Caesar were similar? are the qualities shared by these two figures common to all great political and military leaders or are they unique? are they still important today? why or why not?

RESEARCH TOPICS

Everyone in the class will be assigned the task of preparing a character study of Alexander the Great. Each student will, however, be given a different source upon which to base his or her study.

In your presentation, be sure to address the following issues:
1. How does *your* author describe the personality, strengths and failings of Alexander?
2. What is the picture of Alexander which emerges from this work?
3. How is that picture similar to or different from the view of Alexander which we saw in the film?

You will be asked to use *one* of the following primary or secondary sources:

PRIMARY SOURCE MATERIAL

Arrian, *Life of Alexander* [in translation]
Plutarch, *Life of Alexander* [in translation]

SECONDARY SOURCE MATERIAL

Margarete Bieber, *Alexander the Great in Greek and Roman Art* (Chicago, IL 1964)
E.A. Wallis Budge, *The Life and Exploits of Alexander the Great*, two volumes (London 1968)
Lewis V. Cummins, *Alexander the Great* (Boston, MA 1940)
Robin Lane Fox, *The Search for Alexander the Great* (New York, NY 1980)
J.F.C. Fuller, *The Generalship of Alexander the Great* (London 1958)
G.T. Griffith, *Alexander the Great: The Main Problems* (New York, NY 1966)
N.G.L. Hammond, *Alexander the Great: King, Commander and Statesman* (Park Ridge, NJ 1980)
A.J. Heisserer, *Alexander the Great and the Greeks: The Epigraphic Evidence* (Norman, Oklahoma 1980)
Stephen Krensky, *Conqueror and Hero: The Search for Alexander* (New York, NY: 1981)
Lionel Pearson, *The Lost Histories of Alexander the Great* (New York, NY 1960)
Mary Renault, *Fire From Heaven* (New York, NY 1969)
___, *Funeral Games* (New York, NY 1981)
___, *The Nature of Alexander* (London 1975)
___, *The Persian Boy* (New York, NY 1972)
Charles Alexander Robinson, *Alexander the Great* (New York, NY 1963)
John W. Snyder, *Alexander the Great* (New York 1966)
W.W. Tarn, *Alexander the Great*, two volumes (Cambridge 1950)
C. Bradford Welles, *Alexander and the Hellenistic World* (Toronto 1970)

A Study Guide For: *Alexander the Great*. [Richard Burton]. ©1955 Rossen Films, S.A. Copyright renewed 1983 United Artists Corporation. Distributed on videocassette by MGM/UA Home Video, 1350 Avenue of the Americas, New York, NY, 10019.

VOCABULARY:

Aeschines
Demosthenes
Macedon
Philip [II]
Olympias
Ephesus
Pella
Alexandropolis
Eurydice
Chaeronea
Pausanias
Darius
Granicus
Gordian Knot
Issus
Roxane
Cleitus

1. Which two famous Athenian orators are arguing with one another as the film opens? Which of them violently opposes Philip?
2. What is the name of Alexander's father? What is the name of Alexander's mother?
3. List some of the signs and omens which were said to have occurred at Alexander's birth. What was the location of the temple which was struck by lightning and burned to the ground?
4. How is Olympias described?
5. Which activities were part of Alexander's *physical* education? his *intellectual* education?
6. What was "the choice of Achilles"?
7. Which rank is Alexander assigned in Pella while Philip is away, fighting his enemies?
8. Which city does Alexander cause to be named after him?
9. Which part of Philip's army did Alexander command during the battle against the Athenians?
10. Who was Eurydice?
11. What happened at Chaeronea?
12. Who won the Battle of Chaeronea [338 B.C.]?
13. How did Philip *initially* treat the Athenian dead from the Battle of Chaeronea?
14. Under whose escort did Philip send the ashes of the Athenian dead back to Athens?
15. Which remark especially angered Alexander at Philip's wedding?
16. Who is "the man who was preparing to pass from Europe into Asia but cannot even pass from one couch to another"? Who made this remark? When and where?
17. What was the name of Philip's new wife?
18. Who assassinated Philip? Where?
19. Who was proclaimed king after Philip's death?
20. Which Greek city-state refused to grant allegiance to Alexander?
21. How old was Alexander in 334 B.C.?
22. Who was Darius?
23. What was the outcome of the Battle of Granicus [334 B.C.]?
24. What happened to all of the Greeks who fought on the Persian side during the Battle of Granicus?
25. What was the legend of the Gordian Knot? How did Alexander unravel this knot?
26. What was Alexander's strategy at the Battle of Issus [333 B.C.]?
27. Whom did Alexander discover abandoned by Darius after the Battle of Issus?
28. How did Darius die?
29. Who was Roxane?

30. How did Alexander treat the murderers of Darius?
31. Who killed Cleitus with a spear?
32. What was Alexander's reaction to the death of Cleitus?
33. Whom did Alexander marry at Susa?
34. To whom did Alexander, on his deathbed, leave his empire?

Answer the following questions when the film is over:
1. How would you describe the relationship between Philip and Olympias? between Philip and Alexander?
2. Discuss the character, temperament and personality of each of the following characters: Philip, Olympias, Alexander.
3. Describe the weapons and siege equipment which you saw during the film.
4. How would you describe Alexander's treatment of his troops? his treatment of his fellow officers?
5. Who was Roxane said to be in the movie? Using a classical handbook or an historical summary, try to find out who she really was.
6. In general, how did the Macedonians tend to regard the Persians? How did the Persians tend to regard the Macedonians?

ADDITIONAL DISCUSSION QUESTIONS:
1. Aristotle, Parmenio, Cleitus, and Barsine, while important figures *historically*, tend to be only minor characters in the film. Who were they and what do we learn about them in the movie? What else can you find out about these figures?
2. Which of the qualities and characteristics that you have seen in Philip, Olympias and Alexander may also be found in the character of Julius Caesar? Which of these three characters does Caesar most remember? Why?

Sample Quiz and Examination Questions For *Alexander the Great*

Short Answer

List five important personal qualities which we saw in Alexander the Great. List five such qualities for Julius Caesar. Which qualities appear on *both* of your lists? Which qualities distinguish only one of these generals?

Essay

The ancient biographer Plutarch, at the beginning of his *Life of Alexander*, states that "it is not always in a person's greatest accomplishments that virtues or vices are best perceived; rather it is often an action of small importance, a brief remark, or a jest which will reveal one's character better than the greatest sieges or gravest battles." Using this statement as your topic sentence, write a formal, two-page essay -- free of grammatical and stylistic errors -- which compares and contrasts the characters of Alexander the Great and Julius Caesar. Which actions, remarks and jests reveal the personal qualities of each man? How do these characters turn out to be similar? How do they turn out to be different? Assess the importance of each of the personal qualities which you have listed: what role did they play in the political and military success of Caesar and Alexander? In supporting your remarks, be sure to cite specific episodes from the film *Alexander the Great* and from the text of the *Gallic Wars*.   [50 points]

Take Home Essay

Plutarch frequently ends a section of his *Parallel Lives* with a brief essay comparing and contrasting whichever two important individuals he has just discussed. Thus we have essays by Plutarch entitled "Romulus and Theseus Compared," "Demosthenes and Cicero Compared," and so on. Now, while Plutarch did pair his *Life of Alexander* with his *Life of Julius Caesar*, no separate essay comparing these two great men has come down to us. Write one. Your essay should be approximately two to three pages in length. Use specific examples to illustrate the similarities and differences between these two men. Also be sure to give attention to any similarities which you perceive to have existed in the historical periods during which Caesar and Alexander lived.

Ben-Hur

UNIT TOPIC
A Social History of Rome and the Provinces: A Unit on the Film *Ben-Hur*

UNIT OBJECTIVES
Students of third year Latin will view 1959 film Ben-Hur and consider the information which it contains in order to:
- a] examine the relationship between Rome and its provinces during the early Empire
- b] consider the procedures and social significance of the ancient Roman sport of chariot racing
- c] learn about Roman warfare, especially the strategy and techniques of naval combat

TEACHER ACTIVITIES
1] Before the film:
   - --review with the students what they already know about chariiot racing [the *ludi circenses*], the Roman navy, and the relationship between Rome and its provinces
   - --locate Judaea and Jerusalem on a map
   - --provide a brief history of Judaea since Pompey's conquest of it in 63 B.C. [also have the students try to remember *other* events which occurred in 63 B.C.] and its status as part of the Roman province of Syria
2] After the film is over, review with the students what the movie has taught them movie about:
   - --naval warfare in ancient Rome
   - --chariot racing
   - --leprosy
3] Assign research projects related to the issues raised in the film
4] Translate with the class and discuss the co-ordinated texts [Suetonius *Life of Nero* 22.1-2 and *Life of Vespasian* 4.5-6, Pliny the Younger *Epistles* 9.6]
5] Provide a quiz on the film and co-ordinated readings; discuss the quiz; provide an examination reinforcing the same material
6] Correct and return to each student the study guide, quiz, examination and research project

STUDENT ACTIVITIES
1] Watch the film *Ben-Hur*
2] Complete, fully and correctly, the assigned study guide
3] Participate in all class discussions
4] Translate the co-ordinated texts [Suetonius *Life of Nero* 22.1-2 and *Life of Vespasian* 4.5-6, Pliny the Younger *Epistles* 9.6]
5] Attain a minimum grade of 80 on the quiz
6] Attain a minimum grade of 80 on the examination
7] Complete one of the assigned research projects for a final grade

DISCUSSION TOPICS [FOR CO-ORDINATED TEXTS]

1] Suetonius, *The Life of Nero* 22.1-2
 --who or what were the "Greens" [*prasinum*] which appear in the opening sentence?
 --what happened to the charioteer of the "Greens" who is mentionedby Suetonius? which character in *Ben-Hur* suffered a similar fate? does this accident appear to have been common for ancient charioteers?
 --who was Hector? what did Achilles do to Hector which made him similar to this charioteer of the "Greens"?
 --what is the significance of "dropping the napkin" [*mittente mappam*] which is mentioned at the end of this passage?

2] Pliny the Younger, *Epistles* 9.6
 --what is Pliny's attitude toward chariot racing?
 --does Pliny imply that the races were popular?
 --what, according to Pliny, was the great attraction of these races for most Romans?
 --what does Pliny suggest about the popularity of the races among what he calls "serious people" [*graves homines*]?

3] Suetonius, *The Life of Vespasian* 4.5-6
 --what does this passage reveal about the feelings among the Judaeans towards their the Roman conquerors?
 --how long after the events depicted in *Ben-Hur* is this incident said to have occured?
 --which Roman weapons are mentioned in this passage? which of these weapons did we see in the film?
 --what is the "eagle" [*aquila*] which is mentioned near the beginning of the passage? where did we see one of these "eagles" in the film?
 --how many additional forces are said to have been sent to Judaea in this passage? how many soldiers would there have been in those forces?

RESEARCH TOPICS

1] Chariot Racing
   Begin your research with:
   Carcopino, Jerome. *Daily Life in Ancient Rome*, translated by Henry T. Rowell. New Haven, CT: Yale University Press, 1940. Pages 212-221.
   Carpiceci, Alberto Carlo. *Rome: 2000 Years Ago*, translated by Merry Orling. Florence: Bonechi Edizioni. Pages 121-124.
   Cowell, F.R. *Life in Ancient Rome*. New York, NY: Putnam's, 1961. Pages 171-173.
   dell' Orto, Luisa Franchi. *Ancient Rome: Life and Art*, translated by Carol Wasserman. New York, NY: Scala Books, 1982. Pages 41-45.
   And then use *at least one* of the following:
   Buchanan, David. *Roman Sport and Entertainment*. New York, NY: Longman, 1975.
   Gardiner, E.N. *Athletics in the Ancient World*. Oxford: Oxford University Press, 1955.
   Harris, H.A. *Sport in Ancient Greece and Rome*. London: 1972.

2] Roman Judaea
   Works for the general reader:
   Alpher, Joseph, editor. *The Encyclopedia of Jewish History*.
   Kedouri, Elie. *The Jewish World: History and Culture of the Jewish People*.
   Johnson, Paul. *A History of the Jews*.
   Wurmbrand, Max and Roth, Cecil. *The Jewish People: 4,000 Yearsof Survival*.
   Scholarly works [**NOTE** that these texts should be recommended only to better students]:
   Baron, S.W. *A Social and Religious History of the Jews*. 1952.
   Foerster, Werner. *From the Exile to Christ: A Historical Introduction to Palestinian Judaism*, translated by Gordon E. Harris. 1964.
   Leon, H.J. *The Jews of Ancient Rome*. 1960.
   Tcherikover, V.A. *Hellenistic Civilization and the Jews*. 1959.

3] Naval Warfare
   Casson, Lionel. *Ships and Seamanship in the Ancient World*. Princeton, NJ: Princeton University Press, 1971
   Rodgers, William Ledyard. *Greek and Roman Naval Warfare*. Annapolis, MD: United States Naval Institute, 1964.
   Starr, Chester G. *The Influence of Sea Power on Ancient History*. Oxford: Oxford University Press, 1988.

4] Leprosy
   Herodotus 1.138
   Hippocrates *Aphorisms* 3.20
   Leviticus 13.1-17, 45-49; 14 [entire]
   Numbers 12 [entire]
   Use these ancient sources to write a paper about the attitude towards and "treatment" of leprosy in the ancient world. For a useful summary of medical knowledge in the ancient world, see the General Introduction to Volume I of the Loeb Hippocrates.

A Study Guide For: *Ben-Hur*. [Charlton Heston]. ©1959 Loew's Incorporated. Copyright renewed 1987 Turner Entertainment Co. Distributed on videocassette by MGM/UA Home Video Inc., 1000 Washington Boulevard, Culver City, CA, 90232.

1. How long had Judaea "lain under the mastery of Rome" when the film begins? In what year "of the reign of Augustus Caesar did an imperial decree order every Judaean to return each to his place of birth to be counted and taxed"?
2. Which fortress and seat of Roman power dominated the capital city of Jerusalem?
3. Answer the following questions about the character of Messala:
   --What is his attitude toward the inhabitants of Judaea? Why?
   --What position in the Roman military hierarchy does he assume?
   --How would you describe his initial attitude towards Judah Ben-Hur? How would you describe Ben-Hur's initial attitude toward him?
   --Describe his skill at throwing the javelin. Compare it to that of Ben-Hur. What is the symbolic or thematic significance of this?
   --Whose life did he once save?
   --What is the cause of the antagonism which arises between Messala and Ben-Hur?
4. What does the request which Simonides and Esther make of Ben-Hur indicate to us about marriage customs in Judaea?
5. What does Esther wear as a sign that she is a slave?
6. Describe the objects carried by the officials who proceed the Roman governor as he enters Jerusalem.
7. Why does Messala condemn Ben-Hur even though he knows that he and his family are innocent? What seems to account for this dramatic change in Messala's personality?
8. How is the pace of the rowers maintained in the Roman galley?
9. How many rowers are there on the Roman galley? How many are relieved every hour?
10. Which weapons do we see being used by the Romans during the naval battle? What seems to be the major Roman naval strategy?
11. What is the symbolic or thematic importance of having Ben-Hur and Quintus Arrius drink water soon after they board the Roman ship which saves them?
12. Describe the triumphal procession of Quintus Arrius. How does this procession differ from what you know about Roman triumphs?
13. Which of the sheik's customs seem strange to Ben-Hur?
14. What is the disease that Miriam and Tirzah, Ben-Hur's mother and sister, contract while in prison?

INTERMISSION

1. Which "divine" Roman emperor, currently reigning, is mentioned by the sheik at the baths?
2. Describe the "notebook" which the sheik uses.
3. Which unit of money is mentioned when the wager is made?
4. How many laps around the circus does Ben-Hur mention when speaking to the horses?
5. What object does the sheik give to Ben-Hur just before the race?
6. How many horses are used to draw each chariot?
7. Which deity does Messala invoke just before the race?
8. What signal does Pontius Pilate give to start the race?
9. How are the laps of the race marked?
10. How is Messala injured?

Answer the following questions when the film is over:
1. What was the attitude of the Judaeans towards their Roman rulers? Which factors seem to have accounted for this attitude?
2. Describe the treatment of lepers in the ancient world.
3. What does this movie teach us about ancient Roman warfare?

Sample Quiz and Examination Questions For *Ben-Hur*

Short Answer

In the film *Ben-Hur*, what was the general attitude of the Romans towards the inhabitants of Judaea? Why do the Romans seem to have developed that attitude? How, in turn, did the Jews regard the Romans? What seems to have been the reason for that attitude? Were the major differences between Roman and Jew political in nature? religious? cultural? personal?

Essay

Imagine that you are an ancient Roman attending a chariot race in the Circus Maximus. What would you see? Be specific in your answer, describing not only the physical setting of the Circus Maximus itself but also the day's events in their proper sequence. What would the charioteers wear? Why is this uniform important? What signal is given to start the race? How many laps are there in each race and how are they counted?   [50 points]

Take Home Essay

Translate Martial *Epigrams* 10.50 and 10.53 and then answer the following questions:
1. Who was Scorpus? How did he die? How old was he when he died?
2. Which specific words give us the impression that Scorpus was successful in his career?
3. What *symbolic value* is attached to chariot racing in these poems? [Note especially the words "*nigros . . . equos*" and "*vitae . . . meta tuae*" at 10.50 lines 6 and 8.]
4. Who is Lachesis, mentioned at 10.53.3?
5. What kind of subjunctive are the verbs *frangat* and *mutet* at 10.50 lines 1 and 3?
6. On the basis of these poems, the movie *Ben-Hur*, and our discussions in class, how popular does chariot racing seem to have been in the ancient Roman world?

Cleopatra

UNIT TOPIC

History and Personality in the Late Roman Republic: A Unit on the Film *Cleopatra*

UNIT OBJECTIVES

Students of second year Latin will view the 1963 film *Cleopatra* and consider the information which it contains in order to:
- a] review the historical development of the late Roman Republic
- b] evaluate the contributions made to Roman history by such important figures as Cleopatra, Julius Caesar, Marc Antony, Cicero, M. Junius Brutus, and Octavian
- c] assess the role which these and other major figures played in shaping the course of Roman history

TEACHER ACTIVITIES

1] Before the film, review with the students what they already know about the following historical figures: Cleopatra, Julius Caesar, Marc Antony, and Cicero
   - --what *facts* can the students provide?
   - --what *impressions* do the students have of these figures?
   - --record these facts and impressions on the blackboard and in a notebook for review after the film
2] After the film, remind the students what the movie has shown us about:
   - --the Ptolemaic dynasty of pharoahs
   - --Caesar's attitude toward Catullus and vice versa
   - --the "falling sickness"
   - --the "turtle" [i.e., the tortoise formation or *testudo*]
   - --Roman weapons and the strategy of naval warfare
   - --the battles of Pharsalus, Philippi and Actium
3] Assign research projects related to the issues raised in the film
4] Lead the translation and discussion of the co-ordinated texts [Horace *Odes* 1.37, Vergil *Aeneid* 8.675-731, and Catullus 93]
5] Remind the students of their original statements about Cleopatra, Julius Caesar, Marc Antony, and Cicero
   - --how has this exercise confirmed those original impressions?
   - --how has it altered them?
   - --what additional impressions has it provided of M. Junius Brutus and Octavian?
6] When the students' research projects are well under way, ask the class how well the depictions of each of the major historical figures in the film correspond with what we know about them from other sources
7] Provide a quiz on the film and co-ordinated readings; discuss the quiz; provide an examination reinforcing the same material
8] Correct and return study guide, quiz, examination and research project

STUDENT ACTIVITIES
1] Watch the film *Cleopatra*
2] Complete, fully and correctly, the assigned study guide
3] Participate in all class discussions
4] Translate the co-ordinated texts [Horace *Odes* 1.37, Vergil *Aeneid* 8.675-731, and Catullus 93]
5] Attain a minimum grade of 80 on the quiz
6] Attain a minimum grade of 80 on the examination
7] Complete one of the assigned research projects for a final grade

DISCUSSION TOPICS [FOR CO-ORDINATED TEXTS]

1] Horace *Odes* 1.37
- --review with the students the use of the *passive periphrastic* in Latin as it appears in the opening line
- --discuss the literary device of *anaphora* by pointing out the repetition of *nunc* in the first stanza; which other sounds are repeated in this poem? ["c" in *Caecubum . . . cellis . . . Capitolio* (second stanza); *quae, nec* and *c-* in the sixth stanza; *-um* and *-o* at the end of the last two lines in the seventh and eighth stanzas]; what is the effect of this repetition?
- --what connotation does drinking have in the first stanza? what connotation does it have in the word *ebria* at line 12? in the word *Maeotico* at line 14? in the word *combiberet* at line 28? how might this changing imagery be said to reflect a changing view of Cleopatra herself throughout the poem?
- --what is the dominant image of the fifth stanza?
- --how is Cleopatra's behavior at the Battle of Actium contrasted to her behavior just before her death?
- --after the students have translated the poem, draw their attention to the fact that Antony is not specifically mentioned in it
- --ask the students to suggest reasons why Horace may have chosen to ignore Antony in this work
- --compare this poem to the two surviving lines of Alcaeus' poem concerning the death of the tyrant Myrsilus of Mitylene [Bergk 20, Diehl 39, Lobel and Page 332]; where else have the students seen a Roman borrowing so directly from a Greek lyric poet? [Catullus 51 from Sappho (Bergk 2, Diehl 2, Lobel and Page 31)]
- --describe the picture of Cleopatra which emerges in this poem: is it hostile or admiring or both? how do we sense this?
- --how is this picture similar to or different from the view of Cleopatra which appears in the film?

2] Vergil *Aeneid* 8.675-731
- --explain to the students that this passage is describing a scene on the shield of Aeneas which depicts events occurring in the past as far as Vergil's readers were concerned but which formed part of an unknown future for Aeneas himself
- --how do lines 680-681 affect the reader's view of Caesar and Augustus?
- --what is the image of Antony and Cleopatra that emerges at lines 685-688? how is Cleopatra depicted throughout the passage as a whole?
- --how does the passage represent the Battle of Actium as a struggle between Roman gods and Egyptian gods? what is the effect of this?
- --which words and names does Vergil use to make Egypt and Cleopatra seem exotic or barbaric?

3] Catullus 93
    --read aloud the following passage from Suetonius *Divus Julius* 73:

> *Valerium Catullum, a quo sibi versiculis de Mamurra perpetua stigmata imposita non dissimulaverat, satis facientem eadem die adhibuit cenae hospitioque patris eius, sicut consuerat, uti perseveravit.*

> "[Caesar] freely admitted that Valerius Catullus had permanently tarnished his reputation by writing those verses about Mamurra. Yet when Catullus apologized, Caesar invited him to dinner on that very day and continued his long-standing friendship with Catullus' father."

    --explain that the poems to which Suetonius is referring here, Catullus 29 and 57, are vicious lampoons, attributing a variety of personal and professional improprieties to Caesar and Mamurra
    --discuss the literary device of *litotes* by pointing out the effect of the opening phrase *Nil nimium* . . .
    --what is the relationship between Caesar and Catullus that is suggested by this poem and the passage from Suetonius? how is a similar relationship suggested in the movie?

RESEARCH TOPICS

1. Read Michael Grant's *Cleopatra* [New York, NY: Simon and Schuster, 1972] and then write a paper addressing the following issues: What is the historical accuracy of the film *Cleopatra*? Which events seem actually to have occurred just as they are presented in the film? Which events were altered for the sake of the movie? What are the skills, qualities and abilities that made the historical Cleopatra so important in world history? Are those factors accurately portrayed in the film? Are Cleopatra's relationships with Caesar and Antony accurately portrayed in the film?

2. Read George Bernard Shaw's play *Caesar and Cleopatra*. Then write a paper *comparing* the image of Caesar which appears in this play to that which appears in the film *Cleopatra*. Also *contrast* the two images of Cleopatra. Which version of Cleopatra seems more youthful and innocent? Which seems more worldly and competent? Why, do you believe, is it possible for authors to make such divergent interpretations of the same historical figure?3. Read, in translation, one of the following selections from Plutarch's *Lives*:
    The Life of Julius Caesar
    The Life of Marcus Brutus
    The Life of Marcus Antonius [Marc Antony]
Then write a paper which compares and contrasts the image of the title character which appears in this work to that which appears in the film *Cleopatra*. Is Cleopatra herself mentioned in the work? If so, what do we learn about her? Which other figures appearing in the film are mentioned in the passage of Plutarch which you have read? How does Plutarch's characterization of these figures resemble or differ from what you have seen in the movie?

4. Read one of the following historical novels based upon the life of Cleopatra:

    Claude Ferval, *Cleopatra*, translated by M.E. Poindexter. Garden City, NY: Garden City Publishing Company, 1924.
    Emil Ludwig, *Cleopatra*, translated by Bernard Miall. New York, NY: Viking Press, 1937.

Then write a paper comparing and contrasting the view of Cleopatra (and the other major historical figures of this period) which appears in this novel with that which appears in the 1963 film *Cleopatra*.

5. Read one of the following biographies of Cleopatra:

    Alice Curtis Desmond, *Cleopatra's Children*. New York, NY: 1971.
    Margaret Leighton, *Cleopatra: Sister of the Moon*. New York, NY: 1969.

Then write a paper comparing and contrasting the view of Cleopatra (and the other major historical figures of this period) which appears in this biography with that which appears in the 1963 film *Cleopatra*.

Cleopatra

A Study Guide For: *Cleopatra*. [Elizabeth Taylor]. ©1963 Twentieth Century-Fox Productions, Ltd. Distributed on videocassette by CBS/Fox Video, 39000 Seven Mile Road, Livonia, MI, 48152.

1. Which ancient sources for the life of Cleopatra are mentioned as a basis for this film during the title sequence?
2. What has happened at Pharsalus when the film begins?
3. Where did Pompey go after the Battle of Pharsalus?
4. What do we learn about the attitude of the young Egyptian pharoah, Ptolemy, towards his sister Cleopatra?
5. Whom did Ptolemy's father wish to rule Egypt after his death?
6. How did Caesar learn of Pompey's death?
7. What was Caesar's reaction upon learning of Pompey's death?
8. Which ancient burial customs did Caesar order for Pompey's funeral?
9. How did Cleopatra make her first appearance to Caesar?
10. From which Roman goddess did Caesar claim descent?
11. How did Caesar's daughter die?
12. Whose tomb did Caesar visit during his stay in Egypt?
13. What was Catullus' opinion of Caesar? What was Caesar's opinion of Catullus?
14. What is the "falling sickness"? According to the film, which other famous general[s] had this disease in antiquity?
15. How, according to tradition, was the Library of Alexandria destroyed?
16. What is the "turtle" formation?
17. Whom did many people believe to be Caesar's son?
18. Who was Caesar's fourth wife? How long had they been married by the time of Caesar's stay in Egypt?
19. What did it mean, according to Roman law and tradition, for a father to pick up a newborn child when it had been set at his feet?
20. What did Caesar and Cleopatra name their son?
21. How long did it take Caesar from the time that he left Egypt until he arrived in Rome?
22. What manner of death did Caesar say that he would prefer if he were given the choice?
23. What did Calpurnia do before Caesar left to meet with the senate on the Ides of March in 44 B.C.? What was her dream?
24. To whom did Caesar turn for help when he was stabbed? What was the response?
25. At the foot of whose statue did Caesar fall when he was stabbed?

INTERMISSION

1. Who was victorious at the Battle of Philippi?
2. Who used his own cloak to cover Brutus' body?
3. What seems to have been the general state of Octavian's health?
4. Who were the members of the [Second] Triumvirate? How was the Roman world divided among them?
5. Whom did Octavian want Antony to marry in order to strengthen the bond between them?
6. To which conditions did Marc Antony yield in order to secure Cleopatra's assistance?
7. What were the contents of Antony's will as revealed by Octavian?
8. Where in Greece did the forces of Octavian meet the forces of Antony?
9. Who commanded the naval forces of Octavian?

Cleopatra

10. What did Cleopatra do during the Battle of Actium when it looked as though Antony would be defeated?
11. What was Antony's reaction when he saw Cleopatra's barge retreating from the battle?
12. Why did Octavian want Cleopatra to be taken alive?
13. What happened to Caesarion when he attempted to leave Egypt?
14. How did Antony die? How did Cleopatra die?

Answer the following questions when the film is over:
1. What qualities of Cleopatra as revealed by this film seem best to explain her importance in world history and her influence upon others?
2. Describe the character of Caesar as it is depicted in this film. What were his greatest strengths?
3. Describe the character of Marc Antony as it is depicted in this film. What were his greatest faults?
4. How would you describe the other characters who appear in this film: Cicero? Octavian? Brutus? How do these depictions compare to what we know about these characters from other sources?
5. What, in your opinion, accounts for Caesar's reaction to the news of Pompey's death? How does this compare to Marc Antony's treatment of Brutus after his death?

Sample Quiz and Examination Questions For *Cleopatra*

Short Answer

List the five most important personal qualities of Cleopatra. Do the same for Julius Caesar and Marc Antony. Which of these qualities do you believe most contributed to the success of these figures? Which of these qualities most contributed to their failure? Are there any qualities which can *guarantee* success (or failure)? If so, what are they? If not, what other factors are involved?

Essay

The Greek philosopher Heraclitus once said that "one's character is one's fate" [fragment 119]. This means, in other words, that, according to Heraclitus, our personality determines our destiny. In a formal, two-page essay -- free of grammatical and stylistic errors -- apply this maxim to the lives of Cleopatra, Julius Caesar and Marc Antony. Use specific examples to support each of your points. [50 points]

Take Home Essay

The British author E.M. Forster, in his novel *Alexandria*, described Cleopatra in the following words: "She did not differ in character from the other able and unscrupulous queens of her race, but she had one source of power that they denied themselves -- the power of the courtesan -- and she exploited it professionally. Though passionate she was not the slave of passion, still less of sentimentality. Her safety, and the safety of Egypt were her care; the clumsy and amorous Romans, who menaced both, were her natural prey." In light of what you have learned about Cleopatra in this unit, do you agree with Forster's analysis? In what ways does he correctly describe Cleopatra's nature and her character? In what ways is he incorrect? Use specific examples and illustrations to support your position.

Fall of the Roman Empire

UNIT TOPIC
Assault from Without and Decay from Within: A Unit on the Film *Fall of the Roman Empire*

UNIT OBJECTIVES
Students of first year Latin will view the 1961 film *Fall of the Roman Empire* and consider the information which it contains in order to:
- a] trace the historical developments of the late second century A.D.
- b] evaluate the contributions made to Roman history by Marcus Aurelius and Commodus
- c] identify structures in the Roman Forum, learning about their use and appearance in antiquity
- d] assess those factors which led to the fall of Rome and which can, indeed, lead to the fall of any civilization

TEACHER ACTIVITIES
1] Before the film:
   - --provide a brief history of the Antonine dynasty, identifying both Marcus Aurelius and Commodus
   - --note that the film is *highly* fictionalized, especially in its portrayal of Lucilla [full name: "Annia Aurelia Galeria Lucilla"], pointing out that, in reality, Lucilla was married first to Lucius Verus (who both served as co-emperor with Marcus Aurelius and died before him) and then to Tiberius Claudius Pompeianus (one of Marcus Aurelius' most important commanders)
   - --distribute to the class a map of the Roman Forum as it existed during the Empire: tell the students to use this map to help them identify the structures along the northwest end of the Roman Forum which have been reconstructed in the film
   - --have the students develop a list of factors which, in their opinion, led to the fall of Rome; list these factors on the board or on an overhead transparency as the students record them in their notebooks
2] After the film:
   - --which structures in the Roman Forum did the students observe? [if possible, show the class slides of these structures as they appear now: how different did the Forum look in antiquity from its appearance today?]
   - --read to the class, in translation, Dio Cassius 73.4.4-5 [available in a Loeb edition as *Dio's Roman History*, with a translation by Earnest Cary, in volume IX, pages 77-79]: how is the *character* of Lucilla different in Dio Cassius from the way in which she was portrayed in the film? how are the *facts* of her life different?
   - --mention to the class that the figure of Livius in the film is completely unhistorical
   - --review with the class the list of factors leading to the fall of Rome which they prepared before the film: is there anything which they would now add to this list or remove from it? are these factors a valid "warning" for all civilizations or did they apply specifically to Rome?
3] Assign research projects related to the issues raised in the film
4] Lead the translation and discussion of the co-ordinated texts [*The Last Words of Marcus (Aurelius)* in translation; *Scriptores Historiae Augustae: Commodus Antoninus* 11.10-12; *Scriptores Historiae Augustae: Marcus (Aurelius)*

Antoninus 4.8-10; Marcus Aurelius, *Meditations* [or *To Himself*] 1.5 (in translation)]
5] Provide a quiz on the film and co-ordinated readings; discuss the quiz; provide an examination reinforcing the same material
6] Correct and return study guide, quiz, examination and research project

STUDENT ACTIVITIES
1] Watch the film *Fall of the Roman Empire*
2] Complete, fully and correctly, the assigned study guide
3] Participate in all class discussions
4] Read or translate the co-ordinated texts [*The Last Words of Marcus (Aurelius)* in translation; *Scriptores Historiae Augustae: Commodus Antoninus* 11.10-12; *Scriptores Historiae Augustae: Marcus (Aurelius) Antoninus* 4.8-10; Marcus Aurelius, *Meditations* [or *To Himself*] 1.5 (in translation)]
5] Attain a minimum grade of 80 on the quiz
6] Attain a minimum grade of 80 on the examination
7] Complete one of the assigned research projects for a final grade

DISCUSSION TOPICS [FOR CO-ORDINATED TEXTS]

1] *The Last Words of Marcus [Aurelius]* (in translation) [available in the Loeb edition of Marcus Aurelius Antoninus, translated by C.R. Haines, pages 355-357]
   --note that the "child" or "son" mentioned in this passage is Commodus
   --how does the passage indicate that the attitude of Marcus Aurelius towards Commodus may have been different in reality from the way in which it was depicted in the movie?
   --which statements of Marcus Aurelius foreshadow the later behavior of Commodus?
   --where in the film did we hear a similar view expressed about the proper relationship between a ruler and his subjects?
   --how are the final instructions of Marcus Aurelius to his friends ironic in terms of what occurred later?

2] *Scriptores Historiae Augustae: Commodus Antoninus* 11.10-12
   --the implied subject of this passage is Commodus
   --what is the tense and mood of *acciperet*?
   --identify *indi*
   --note that *pugnasse* is a shortened form of *pugnavisse*
   --what does this passage suggest about Commodus' attitude towards gladiators and gladiatorial combats?

3] *Scriptores Historiae Augustae: Marcus [Aurelius] Antoninus* 4.8-10
   --the implied subject of this passage is Marcus Aurelius
   --review the ablative of description as it is used in the phrase *tanta indulgentia*
   --what type of clause is *ut cogeretur . . .* ?
   --discuss the chiastic order present in the phrase *verecundus sine ignavia, sine tristitia gravis*
   --what does this passage reveal about the character and interests of Marcus Aurelius? how were his character and interests different from those of Commodus?

4] Marcus Aurelius, *Meditations* [or *To Himself*] 1.5 (in translation)
   --what attitude toward chariot-racing and gladiatorial combat does Marcus Aurelius claim to have received from his tutor?
   --how is this attitude different from that of Commodus?
   --how are the *other* lessons which Marcus Aurelius claimed to have learned from his tutor also different from the beliefs and practices of Commodus?

RESEARCH TOPICS

1. The Fall of the Roman Empire
    Read Bryce Dale Lyon's *The Origins of the Middle Ages* (New York, NY: Norton, 1972) and then write a paper which addresses the following issues: what reasons for the decline of Roman civilization have been suggested by scholars over the years? how was the fall of Rome viewed by Petrarch? by Erasmus? by Edward Gibbon? by J.B. Bury? by Henri Pirenne? what importance to the fall of Rome have these scholars placed on matters such as race, religion and climate? which explanation(s) for the fall of Rome do you believe to be most convincing? why?

2. Gibbon's *Decline and Fall of the Roman Empire*
    How did Edward Gibbon account for the decline and fall of Rome? What role, according to Gibbon, did religion play in this decline? What influences, in his own age and earlier, led Gibbon to this view? How might Gibbon's theory be viewed as reflecting the perspectives and attitudes of his own era?

   In preparing your report, consult *at least one* of the following works:
     Sir Gavin de Beer, *Gibbon and his World* (New York, NY: Viking, 1968).
     E.J. Oliver, *Gibbon and Rome* (New York, NY: Sheed and Ward, 1958).

   With regard to the matter of religion, be sure to read Gibbon's own second chapter in the *Decline and Fall*; you may also wish to consult: Shelby Thomas McCloy, *Gibbon's Antagonism to Christianity* (London: Williams and Norgate, 1933)

3. Economic and Military Causes of Decline
    Read Paul M. Kennedy's *The Rise and Fall of the Great Powers* (New York, NY: Random House, 1987). Then write a paper applying the issues addressed in that book to the Roman Empire. Though the book is concerned only with modern powers, to what extent is its thesis applicable to the ancient world? How were the factors which led to the rise and fall of Roman power similar to those affecting later empires? How were they different?

Fall of the Roman Empire

A Study Guide For: *The Fall of the Roman Empire*. [Sophia Loren]. ©1961 Samuel Bronston Productions Inc. Distributed on videocassette by United Entertainment Inc., 6535 East Skelly Drive, Tulsa, OK, 74145.

1. How many years did it take Rome to fall?
2. Who was emperor in the year 180 A.D.?
3. Who is Commodus?
4. To which goddess is Lucilla praying for peace?
5. On which two borders did the Romans face hostility during the reign of Marcus Aurelius?
6. Who succeeded Marcus Aurelius as emperor?
7. The official who is standing behind Commodus says something to him as he leaves the chariot following his triumphal enry into Rome. What does he say?
8. Which god's temple does Commodus visit after his triumphal entry into Rome? [You should be able to tell by reading the inscription on the statue base.] What does Commodus dedicate to the god in this temple?
9. Whose son is Commodus *really* said to be? [Might there be any truth to this rumor? After the film, read "Marcus Antoninus Aurelius" 19.1-9 in the *Historia Augusta* (pages 126-127 in the Penguin volume, *Lives of the Later Caesars*).]
10. How does Commodus die in the movie? [How did he really die? If you do not know, check a classical handbook or historical summary when the film is over.]

Answer the following questions when the film is over:

1. Look up the answers to the second parts of questions 9 and 10 above.
2. Describe the funeral rites performed for Marcus Aurelius.
3. Describe the clothing worn by the Roman senators throughout the film.
4. How does an empire fall or die? [Review, if necessary, the following scenes from the film: the very beginning; the very end; the meeting at which the Senate decides the fate of the Germans.] What reasons are suggested, in the film, for the fall of the Roman Empire?

Sample Quiz and Examination Questions For *Fall of the Roman Empire*

Short Answer

List five factors which led to the fall of Rome. Which of these factors was or were already present in Roman history during the reign of Commodus? Which of your five factors are general "warning signs" for the fall of any great power? Which are specific to Rome?

Essay

The modern Greek poet Constantine Cavafy once said: "One thing the student of imperial Rome should have in view is that the miserable situation in the capital doesn't at all imply the same situation in the state in general. For one thing, the slowness and difficulty of communications, and for another the good and orderly organization of the different parts of the Roman state, often brought it about that a bad emperor, who did harm in Rome, did none in the provinces." [Quoted by Robert Liddell in *Cavafy: A Biography* (New York, NY: Schocken Books, 1974) 172.] In a formal, three page essay -- free from grammatical and stylistic errors -- respond to Cavafy's statement. Does it seem to be true? Does it seem to be true *with reference to Commodus*? If Cavafy is correct, is this one of the reasons why the fall of Rome was so long in coming? If the effect of a bad emperor upon the provinces was so small, what *did* cause Rome to fall?   [50 points]

Take Home Essay

In *The Decline and Fall of the Roman Empire*, Edward Gibbon defined what he believed to be the greatest age in human history: "If any man were called to fix the period in the history of the world during which the condition of the human race was most happy and prosperous, he would, without hesitation, name that which elapsed from the death of Domitian to the accession of Commodus." Which aspects of the reign of Commodus made this period different from earlier Roman history? Which tendencies and traits, though always present in Roman society, became intensified during this same period? Is it justifiable to claim that, with the death of Marcus Aurelius, the fall of the Roman Empire had already begun?

A Funny Thing Happened on the Way to the Forum

UNIT TOPIC
Comedy Tonight: A Unit on Type Characters and Comic Technique in the Film *A Funny Thing Happened on the Way to the Forum*

UNIT OBJECTIVES
Students of second year Latin will view the 1966 film *A Funny Thing Happened on the Way to the Forum*, considering its plot structure and characters, in order to:
- a] understand the role of "type characters" in ancient Roman comedy and the contribution of these characters to Plautus' comic technique
- b] appreciate the works of Plautus and Terence, while learning about the similarities and differences of these two playwrights
- c] assess the importance of comedy as a form of literature in ancient Rome

TEACHER ACTIVITIES
1] Before the film:
   - --provide a brief summary of Plautus' life and career
   - --characterize the style of comedy written by Plautus and how that style of comedy is reflected in the film
   - --describe what a "type character" is and mention the appearance of these characters in other kinds of comedy [for instance, the *Commedia dell' arte* and the plays of Shakespeare]
2] After the film, analyze each of the characters individually:
   - --how would the class describe each character?
   - --what motivated each character?
   - --how did each character, in the end, get what he or she was looking for (more or less)?
   - --how was each character a fool in his or her own way?
3] Discuss once again the *style* of comedy which appeared in the film:
   - --what made the movie funny?
   - --was the comedy refined? slapstick? satirical? intellectual?
   - --are there any parallels to this style of comedy today?
4] Assign research projects related to the issues raised in the film
5] Lead the translation and discussion of the co-ordinated texts [Livy 7.2; Plautus *Pseudolus* 445-448 and 575-582; Plautus *Miles Gloriosus* 88-94]
6] Provide a quiz on the film and co-ordinated readings; discuss the quiz; provide an examination reinforcing the same material
7] Correct and return study guide, quiz, examination and research project

STUDENT ACTIVITIES
1] Watch the film *A Funny Thing Happened on the Way to the Forum*
2] Complete, fully and correctly, the assigned study guide
3] Participate in all class discussions
4] Translate the co-ordinated texts [Livy 7.2; Plautus *Pseudolus* 445-448 and 575-582; Plautus *Miles Gloriosus* 88-94]
5] Attain a minimum grade of 80 on the quiz
6] Attain a minimum grade of 80 on the examination
7] Complete one of the assigned research projects for a final grade

DISCUSSION TOPICS [FOR CO-ORDINATED TEXTS]

1] Livy 7.2
- --the year is 364 B.C.: who were the consuls for that year?
- --what is a *lectisternium*? how frequently do they seem to have occurred in Roman history?
- --why, according to Livy, were "stage plays" [*ludi scenici*] first instituted in the city of Rome?
- --how does Livy characterize the Roman people living at that time?
- --was drama, according to Livy, a native, Roman creation?
- --from where did the first "actors" [*ludiones*] come to Rome?
- --which musical instrument was used to accompany these early performances?
- --from what people, according to Livy, did the Romans adopt the term "*histriones*"? [what English word(s) do we get from this root?]
- --how does Livy characterize the "Fescennine farces" [*Fescinnino versu*]?
- --what were *saturae*?
- --who was Livius [Andronicus]? what contribution did he make towards the production of plays? why did he stop acting in them?
- --what were the *exodia*?
- --what were the "Atellan farces" [*fabellis Atellanis*]? What people originated them? how was the social status of those who acted in Atellan farces different from those who acted in other types of drama?
- --what does the last sentence imply about drama in Livy's own time?
- --given the origin of Roman drama as a form of "escapism" arising during a time of disaster, how do you believe that this affected the sort of plays which resulted? what affect might this origin have had on the Roman comedies which were produced later?

2] Plautus, *Pseudolus* 445-448, 575-582
- --what is the image of Pseudolus that emerges in these two passages?
- --in what way is this characterization similar to that which we see in *A Funny Thing Happened on the Way to the Forum*? in what way is it different?

3] Plautus, *Miles Gloriosus* 88-94
- --*ille miles* is the title character: how does the speaker [Palaestrio] characterize him?
- --in what way is this characterization similar to that of the Miles Gloriosus whom we see in *A Funny Thing Happened on the Way to the Forum*}? in what way is it different?
- --review the phenomenon of *aphaeresis* in "*conditumst*" and "*stultitiast*" in the *Pseudolus* passages, "*illest*" and "*deridiculost*" in the *Miles Gloriosus* passages

RESEARCH TOPICS

1] Read, in translation, one of the following comedies by Plautus. Then identify which characters or plot elements were borrowed from it for *A Funny Thing Happened on the Way to the Forum*. In addition, note whatever general similarities there are between the comedic style and technique seen in of the play which you have read and that in the movie.

        Casina
        Pseudolus
        Miles Gloriosus [The Braggart Warrior]
        Mostellaria [The Haunted House]

Where does the play which you have read take place? Where does *A Funny Thing Happened on the Way to the Forum* take place?

2] Read, in translation, any of the six surviving comedies of Terence. What is similar about the comedic style and technique of this play and the passages of Plautus which we have read in class? What is different? Using a standard reference work, such as handbook of classical literature, see if you can account for some of the differences between the comedies of Plautus and Terence.

3] The Greek playwright Menander inspired Plautus in much the same way that Plautine comedy inspired *A Funny Thing Happened on the Way to the Forum*. As a result, read, in translation, one of the following plays by Menander. How close in spirit does it seem to be to the Roman comedy which we have read? Using a standard reference work, such as handbook of classical literature, see if you can determine what the general scholarly opinion is about the degree of similarity between Menander and Plautus.

        Dyscolus [The Curmudgeon]
        Epitrepontes [The Arbitration]
        Samia [The Girl from Samos]

4] Read Erich Segal, *Roman Laughter*, second edition. Oxford: Oxford University Press, 1968 and 1987. How does Segal account for the ancient popularity of Plautus?

5] Read K. MacLeish, *Roman Comedy*. Lynchburg, VA: Bristol Classical Press, 1986. What does Roman comedy tell us about *daily life* in the ancient Roman world?

A Study Guide For: *A Funny Thing Happened On The Way To The Forum*. [Zero Mostel]. ©1966 Quadrangle Films and United Artists Corporation. Distributed on videocassette by Twentieth Century-Fox Video, Industrial Park Drive, Farmington Hills, MI, 48024.

THE CHARACTERS:

Senex	a Roman citizen
Domina	the wife of Senex
Hero	the son of Senex
Pseudolus	Hero's clever slave
Hysterium	a good slave from the house of Senex
Marcus Lycus	a buyer and seller of courtesans
Philia	a recent arrival to the house of Lycus
Miles Gloriosus	a swaggering captain of soldiers
Erronius	a befuddled old man in search of his children, stolen in infancy by pirates

1. In how many houses do the principal characters live?
2. What sort of vehicles are used to transport Senex, Domina and Marcus Lycus at the beginning of the film?
3. For what is Pseudolus saving money?
4. Describe the make-up worn by Domina, the wife of Senex.
5. According to Hero's tutor, how many planets exist?
6. Contrast the clothing worn by Pseudolus to that worn by Hero.
7. What name is given to the courtesan who is dressed in many small bells? [Why is this name appropriate?]
8. What name is given to the twin courtesans? [Why is this name appropriate?]
9. From which Greek island did Philia, Hero's beloved, come?
10. What stratagem is used by Pseudolus to get Philia out of the house of Lycus?
11. Describe the lyre which Hero plays.
12. Which goddess, according to Hero, brought the two lovers together only to part them?
13. Watch the movie carefully during the song "Everybody Ought to Have a Maid," and then answer the following questions:
    --what sort of domestic activities do we see being performed?
    --what sort of painting adorns the walls of the house?
    --what is the difference between the footwear worn by the slaves and that worn by the citizens?
14. At which temple does Philia propose to offer herself to the gods? When we finally see this temple, what shape is it?
15. How realistic is the final scene in which all of the difficulties are resolved?

Answer the following questions when the film is over:
1. Give at least one example of each of the following comic devices as they appear in *A Funny Thing Happened On The Way To The Forum*:
    slapstick
    word play
    mistaken identity
    the comic stratagem
    the running gag
2. Contrast the characters of the two slaves, Pseudolus and Hysterium.
3. Describe the following characters in one or two words each: Erronius, Hero, Miles Gloriosus, Senex, Domina, Philia
4. How would you describe twists and turns of plot in this story: as complicated or as simple?
5. Replay the opening scene of the movie in which the song "Comedy Tonight" is sung for the first time. What scenes of "everyday life" in Rome do we observe?
6. What are the various modes of transportation used by the characters in this film?
7. Describe the master-slave relationship that we see in this film. Is this a realistic portrayal of slavery in ancient Rome?
8. Describe the slave market which we see in this film.
9. How might you argue that *all* of the major characters in this story are fools in their own ways?

Sample Quiz and Examination Questions For *A Funny Thing Happened on the Way to the Forum*

Short Answer

Match the name of the character from *A Funny Thing Happened on the Way to the Forum* to that character's "literary type."

____ 1] Pseudolus	a) braggart soldier
____ 2] Erronius	b) good slave
____ 3] Hero	c) befuddled old man
____ 4] Miles Gloriosus	d) tyrannical wife
____ 5] Senex	e) clever slave
____ 6] Hysterium	f) young man in love
____ 7] Philia	g) henpecked husband
____ 8] Domina	h) courtesan with the "heart of gold"

Essay

It is frequently said that the works of Shakespeare contain at least one ingredient for every element of the audience: bawdy humor for the masses; poetry for the intellectuals; romance for the young, and so on. In *A Funny Thing Happened on the Way to the Forum*, the song "Comedy Tonight" suggests that Roman comedy also had "something for everyone." Is it true that the plays of Plautus and Terence would have appealed to all Romans regardless of class and education? If so, what were the elements which would have produced that appeal? If not, which features were missing from Roman comedy and why? In justifying your position, use specific examples from the plays which we have discussed in class.   [50 points]

Take Home Essay

Thomas Carlyle, in *Sartor Resartus*, called laughter "the cipher-key wherewith we decipher the whole man." By this Carlyle meant that we may obtain an excellent insight into a person's psychology by noting the things which make that person laugh. On the basis of what you have learned in this unit, what sort of things made the ancient Romans laugh? What insight does that give us into their personalities?

Masada

UNIT TOPIC
Irreconcilable Differences: A Unit on the Film *Masada*

UNIT OBJECTIVES
Students of fourth year Latin will view the 1980 film *Masada* and consider the information which it contains in order to:
- a] improve their understanding of the conflicts which occurred between Rome and its provinces
- b] review the history of the first century A.D.
- c] appreciate the contribution which engineering played in Roman military campaigns
- d] assess, as objectively as possible, whether the conquest of the provincial territories by Rome was justified

TEACHER ACTIVITIES
1] Before the film:
   - --locate Judaea and Jerusalem on a map
   - --provide a brief history of Judaea since Pompey's conquest of it in 63 B.C. [also have the students try to remember *other* events which occurred in 63 B.C.] and its status for most of the time since then as part of the Roman province of Syria
   - --identify Vespasian, clarifying his role in the Jewish Wars, and (if possible) show the class slides of the reliefs from the Arch of Titus depicting the fall of Jerusalem
   - --define the term "zealots"
2] After the film is over, review with the students what the movie has taught them movie about:
   - --the role of engineering in a Roman conquest
   - --Roman and Hebrew dress
   - --some of the reasons for the fierce Jewish resistance to Roman rule [why did the Romans feel that they could not simply ignore the zealots on Masada? why did the Jews feel that they could not come to terms with the Romans?]
3] Assign research projects related to the issues raised in the film
4] Lead the class in a discussion of the co-ordinated text [Flavius Josephus *Bellum Judaicum* 7.252-402 (in translation)]
5] Provide a quiz on the film and co-ordinated readings; discuss the quiz; provide an examination reinforcing the same material
6] Correct and return to each student the study guide, quiz, examination and research project

STUDENT ACTIVITIES
1] Watch the film *Masada*
2] Complete, fully and correctly, the assigned study guide
3] Participate in all class discussions
4] Read and discuss the co-ordinated text [Flavius Josephus *Bellum Judaicum* 7.252-402 (in translation)]
5] Attain a minimum grade of 80 on the quiz
6] Attain a minimum grade of 80 on the examination
7] Complete one of the assigned research projects for a final grade

DISCUSSION TOPICS [FOR THE CO-ORDINATED TEXT]

Flavius Josephus *Bellum Judaicum* 7.252-402 (in translation) [available in the Loeb edition or as pages 461-476 of the Everyman's Library edition, entitled *Flavius Josephus: The Wars of the Jews*, translated by Jacob Hart (New York, NY: E.P. Dutton, 1915)]

1. How did Flavius Josephus come to be procurator in Judaea?
2. How is Eleazar described?
3. What did Silva build around the fortress at Masada?
4. Were sources of food and water for the Roman army available near to Masada itself?
5. Why was one of the approaches to Masada called "the Serpent Path"? How is this path described?
6. What structures did King Herod build at Masada? What arrangements did he make for water at Masada?
7. Describe the provisions for food and weapons which King Herod made at Masada.
8. Against which enemy had Herod fortified Masada?
9. Describe the ramp or bank built by Flavius Silva.
10. Describe the siege tower built by Flavius Silva.
11. Describe the second wall built by the Jews at the point where the original wall had been breached by the Roman battering ram. Why did the Jews build the new wall in the manner that they did? What did the Romans do in response? What effect did the wind have upon this plan?
12. What were the arguments used by Eleazar in his speech urging the Jews to commit suicide rather than submit to the Romans? What did Eleazar urge the Jews to do with their wealth? What did he urge them to do with their provisions?
13. What was the principle argument which Eleazar then used to persuade those who had still remained hesitant after his initial speech?
14. What means did the Jews use to accomplish their mass suicide?
15. How many Jews survived on Masada? How many perished?
16. What did the Romans see and find upon entering Masada?
17. How did the Romans (and hence Josephus) learn what had happened, and what Eleazar had said, during the last night of the siege?
18. What was the Roman reaction upon learning what the zealots had done?

RESEARCH TOPICS

1. The site of Masada.

   Begin your research with pages 1-20 of Ronald Sanders, *Israel: The View from Masada* (New York, NY: Harper and Row, 1966).

   Then consult Yigael Yadin, *Masada: Herod's Fortress and the Zealot's Last Stand*, translated by Moshe Pearlman (New York, NY: Random House, 1966).

   Be sure to give attention to the issue of how the archaeological remains at Masada complement the historical record in helping us to understand what happened during the Roman siege.

2. The conflict between Roman and Jew in antiquity.

   David Daube, *Civil Disobedience in Antiquity* (Edinburgh: Edinburgh University Press, 1972).
   Richard A. Horsley, *Jesus and the Spiral of Violence: Popular Jewish Resistance in Roman Palestine* (San Francisco, CA: Harper and Row, 1987).
   Lee I. Levine, *Caesarea Under Roman Rule* (Leiden: Brill, 1975).
   Arnaldo Momigliano, *On Pagans, Jews, and Christians*(Middletown, CN: Wesleyan University Press, 1987).
   Marcel Simon, *Verus Israel: A Study of the Relations Between Christians and Jews in the Roman Empire, 135-425*, translated by H. McKeating (New York, NY: Oxford University Press, 1986).
   John E. Stambaugh and David L. Balch, *The New Testament in its Social Environment* (Philadelphia, PA: Westminster Press, 1986).
   Molly Whittaker, *Jews and Christians: Graeco-Roman Views* (New York, NY: Cambridge University Press, 1984).

A Study Guide For: *Masada*. [Peter O'Toole]. ©1980 by Universal City Studios Inc. Distributed on videocassette by MCA Home Video, 70 Universal City Plaza, Universal City, CA, 91608.

1. Answer the following questions about the material which appears in the "scroll" that is seen after the credits. [**NOTE**: the text moves very quickly at this point and it may need to be repeated several times in order for all of the questions to be answered.]
    - --during which century does this story take place?
    - --which legion sacked the city of Jerusalem?
    - --how many men, women and children did the Jews have on Masada?
    - --about how many men did the Romans bring to assault the fortress?
2. Who is emperor of Rome during the conquest of Judaea?
3. From whom did the current emperor take the throne?
4. For how many years has Silva been in Judaea trying to conquer the territory?
5. Which weapons are used by the Jews in their defense of Masada?
6. Whom did the Romans force to build their assault ramp in order to avoid being attacked by the Jews on Masada?
7. In which Egyptian city was Sheva born?
8. Why had the Essenes refused to fight before this?
9. How did the Jews on Masada reinforce the wall at the point where the battering ram was stationed?
10. What did the Romans find when they entered Masada?

Answer the following questions when the film is over:
1. Contrast the dress of the Romans and the Jews.
2. Contrast the weaponry of the Romans and the Jews.
3. Describe the engineering and surveying equipment seen in this film.

Sample Quiz and Examination Questions For *Masada*

Short Answer

Why did the Romans feel that they could not afford simply to ignore the Jews on Masada? Why did the Jews feel that they could not afford to come to terms with the Romans? Does a conflict between these two cultures seem to have been inevitable? If so, why? If not, then why did the conflict occur?

Essay

In what way does the Jewish conflict with the Romans seem typical of other conflicts between conquered peoples living in the Roman provinces and the imperial power which subjugated them? In what way was the Jewish rebellion unique? In preparing your answer to this question, consider the sources of the problem: to what extent was the struggle between Roman and Jew a political struggle? a religious struggle? a racial struggle? a cultural struggle? Does it seem to have been possible for the Jews to have been assimilated into the Roman empire and yet retain their cultural identity? If so, why did the zealots not accept this? If not, what was it about Jewish culture that was irreconcilable with Roman culture?   [50 points]

Take Home Essay

In 1978, more than nine hundred members of the People's Temple committed suicide or were killed in a commune at Jonestown, Guyana. The similarities in the number of people who died and in the religious nature of the two communities have frequently caused this incident to be compared to the mass suicide at Masada. But while the Jews at Masada are usually portrayed as leading a heroic resistance and resorting to suicide only when no other option was possible, those who died at Jonestown are often described as tragic "victims," innocent people who were duped by an egotistical and possibly insane leader. What accounts for the difference between these two impressions? Have we simply obtained greater historical "distance" from the events at Masada or is some other factor at work here? Do the differences between Eleazar and Jim Jones, the leaders of the two groups, explain the different interpretations given to the two events? How has Josephus' portrayal of the events at Masada affected all later views of what happened there? Did Josephus' Jewish ancestry cause him to have greater sympathy for the zealots than for their Roman besiegers? In the case of Jonestown, did the media (television, photographs, and tape recordings) simply bring home more forcefully the horror of an event rather similar to Masada? [If you are uncertain about the answers to some of these questions, research the Jonestown tragedy in an encyclopedia or almanac before beginning your response. You may also wish to examine some of the news stories appearing in magazines and newspapers shortly after the Jonestown disaster itself. Do any of these stories mention Masada? In what connection or making what parallels?]

Spartacus

UNIT TOPIC
Gladiators, Slaves and Slave Revolts: A Unit on the Film *Spartacus*

UNIT OBJECTIVES
Students of first year Latin will view the 1960 film Spartacus and consider the information which it contains in order to improve their understanding of:
- a] gladiatorial combat as a "sport" and social institution in ancient Rome
- b] slavery and the attitude toward slaves in ancient Rome
- c] slave rebellions, especially the revolt of Spartacus which occurred in 73-71 B.C.
- d] the historical figure of Spartacus and his treatment in ancient and modern literature

TEACHER ACTIVITIES
1] Before the film:
   - --review with the students what they already know about gladiators and gladiatorial combat, slavery in the ancient world, Roman civilian and military dress
   - --locate on a map Greece, Thrace, Rome, Capua, Metapontum and Brundisium
   - --spell "Silesia" on the blackboard and locate Silesia in eastern Germany on a map [because of the reference to "Silesian pirates" in the film]; spell "Cilicia" on the blackboard and locate Cilicia in Asia Minor on a map [tell the students that the film is in error: the pirates harassing the Romans in this period were from Cilicia not Silesia; why were the Cilicians more likely to be pirates than Silesians anyway?]
   - --briefly identify the Roman historical figures mentioned in the film: Crassus, Julius Caesar, Pompey
2] After the film is over, review with the students what the movie has taught them movie about:
   - --gladiatorial combat
   - --Roman slavery
   - --Roman warfare
   - --the standards born by legionary soldiers
   - --crucifixion as a Roman punishment
3] Assign research projects related to the issues raised in the film
4] Translate with the class and discuss the co-ordinated texts [Plutarch *Crassus* 8-11 (in translation), Seneca *Epistles* 7.2-5, Cato the Elder *De Agri Cultura* 2.4,7]
5] Provide a quiz on the film and co-ordinated readings; discuss the quiz; provide an examination reinforcing the same material
6] Correct and return to each student the study guide, quiz, examination and research project

STUDENT ACTIVITIES
1] Watch the film *Spartacus*
2] Complete, fully and correctly, the assigned study guide
3] Participate in all class discussions
4] Read or translate the co-ordinated texts [Plutarch *Crassus* 8-11 (in translation), Seneca *Epistles* 7.2-5, Cato the Elder *De Agri Cultura* 2.4,7]
5] Attain a minimum grade of 80 on the quiz
6] Attain a minimum grade of 80 on the examination
7] Complete one of the assigned research projects for a final grade

DISCUSSION TOPICS [FOR CO-ORDINATED TEXTS]

1] Plutarch, *Crassus* 8-11 [in translation]
--Describe the personality of Crassus as Plutarch presents it. How is this presentation of Crassus similar to the one which we see in the film? How is this different?
--Which historical figures mentioned by Plutarch also appear in the film? Which characters in the movie do not appear in Plutarch?
--Why, according to Plutarch, had the men been forced to serve as gladiators?
--How is Spartacus himself described by Plutarch? Is this similar to the picture of him which emerges in the film?
--How is Spartacus' wife described by Plutarch? Is this similar to the picture of her which emerges in the film?
--What does Plutarch give as the name of the praetor who is sent against Spartacus? How many men did he take with him? In the film, this character is described as the "commander of the Roman garrison." What name does he have in the film? How many cohorts did he take with him?
--In which direction is Spartacus heading in Plutarch's account? How does this differ from the direction in which he is heading in the film?
--How did Crassus punish the first five hundred of Mummius' men for their cowardice?
--Where did Spartacus hope to go with the Cilician pirates? Is this the same destination that is mentioned in the film?
--Which generals did Crassus request the Senate to recall from Thrace and Spain? Are these the same generals who are mentioned as coming to Crassus' aid in the movie?
--What did Spartacus do to his horse before the final climactic battle with Crassus? Why?
--How, according to Plutarch, did Spartacus die? How did Spartacus die in the movie? Why, do you suppose, did the film-makers change this element of the plot?

2] Seneca, *Epistles* 7.2-5 [*Nihil vero tam damnosum* through *ne nihil agatur*]
--What effect does Seneca say that attendance at the gladiatorial games has upon his mood and character?
--What kind of show was the "midday spectacle" [*meridianum spectaculum*] which Seneca witnessed? What about it so horrified him?
--What kind of show took place in the morning [*Mane*]?
--How does Seneca describe the reaction of the crowds to these displays?

3] Cato the Elder, *De Agri Cultura* 2.4,7

Cum servi aegrotarint, cibaria tanta dari non oportuisse.... Boves vetulos, armenta delicula, oves deliculas, lanam, pelles, plostrum vetus, ferramenta vetera, SERVUM SENEM, SERVUM MORBOSUM, et siquid aliut supersit, vendat.

--What attitude towards slaves is revealed by Cato's remarks here?
--Does this appear to have been a common Roman attitude? [You may wish to contrast the view expressed at Seneca *Epistles* 47, for instance.]

RESEARCH TOPICS

1. Roman slavery and slave revolts.
    Begin your research with:
    >Carcopino, Jérôme. *Daily Life in Ancient Rome*, translated by Henry T. Rowell. New Haven, CT: Yale University Press, 1940. Pages 56-61.
    >Cowell, F.R. *Life in Ancient Rome*. New York, NY: Putnam's, 1961. Pages 95-110.
    >Baldwin, Barry. "Two Aspects of the Spartacus Slave Revolt." *Classical Journal* 62 (1967) 289-294.

    And then use *at least one* of the following:
    >Barrow, R.H. *Slavery in the Roman Empire*. London: 1928.
    >Duff, A.M. *Freedmen in the Early Roman Empire*. Oxford: Oxford University Press, 1928.
    >Finley, M.I., editor. *Classical Slavery*. London: Frank Cass, 1987.
    >_____, *Slavery in Classical Antiquity*. London: Heffer, 1960.
    >Hopkins, Keith. *Conquerors and Slaves*. Cambridge: Cambridge University Press, 1978.
    >MacMullen, Ramsey. *Enemies of the Roman Order*. Cambridge, MA: Harvard University Press, 1967.
    >Vogt, Joseph. *Ancient Slavery and the Ideal of Man*, translated by Thomas Wiedemann. Oxford: Oxford University Press, 1974.
    >Watson, Alan. *Roman Slave Law*. Baltimore, MD: Johns Hopkins University Press, 1987.
    >Wiedemann, T.E.J. *Slavery*. Oxford: Clarendon Press, 1987.

2. Gladiators and amphitheaters.
    Begin your research with:
    >Carcopino, Jérôme. *Daily Life in Ancient Rome*, translated by Henry T. Rowell. New Haven, CT: Yale University Press, 1940. Pages 231-247.
    >Carpiceci, Alberto Carlo. *Pompeii: 2000 Years Ago*, translated by Michael Hollingworth. Florence: Bonechi Edizioni, 1985. Pages 92-94.
    >_____, *Rome: 2000 Years Ago*, translated by Merry Orling. Florence: Bonechi Edizioni. Pages 64-73.
    >Cowell, F.R. *Life in Ancient Rome*. New York, NY: Putnam's, 1961. Pages 173-179.
    >dell' Orto, Luisa Franchi. *Ancient Rome: Life and Art*, translated by Carol Wasserman. New York, NY: Scala Books, 1982. Pages 45-52.

    And then use *at least one* of the following:
    >Buchanan, David. *Roman Sport and Entertainment*. New York, NY: Longman, 1975.
    >Grant, Michael. *Gladiators*. New York, NY: Delacorte Press, 1967.
    >Pearson, John. *Arena: The Story of the Colosseum*. New York, NY: McGraw-Hill, 1973.

3. The character of Spartacus.
    Read the following two historical novels:
    >Fast, Howard. *Spartacus*. New York, NY: Crown Publishers, 1951.
    >Koestler, Arthur. *The Gladiators*, translated by Edith Simon. New York, NY: Macmillan, 1939, 1965.

    Be sure to address the following issues in your project: how is Fast's interpretation of Spartacus radically different from that of Koestler? How is it possible for two authors to take such divergent views of the same historical figures? Upon which of the novels was the film *Spartacus* based?

4. Warfare in ancient Rome.
>Marsden, Eric William. *Greek and Roman Artillery*. Oxford: Clarendon Press, 1969.
>Watson, G.R. *The Roman Soldier*. London: Thames and Hudson, 1969.
>Webster, Graham. *The Roman Imperial Army*. London: Adam and Charles Black, 1969, 1979.

A Study Guide For: *Spartacus*. [Kirk Douglas]. ©1960 Universal International and Bryna Productions. Distributed on videocassette by MCA Home Video, 70 Universal City Plaza, Universal City, CA, 91608.

1. In which century does this story take place?
2. In which conquered Greek province was Spartacus born?
3. What is a "ceremonial *cauda*"? [After the movie, use a Latin dictionary to find out what the word *cauda* literally means.]
4. In which Italian city is the gladiatorial school located?
5. Which famous Roman general comes to visit the gladiatorial school? [Give all three of his names.]
6. What do the gladiators say before their combat begins?
7. How is Spartacus armed for his first combat? How is the other gladiator armed?
8. Describe the togas and tunics worn by the senators in the Curia.
9. Where are Pompey and his legions said to be? [After the movie, use a historical summary or classical handbook to determine *why* he was there.]
10. How does Crassus learn the skills which his new slaves have been taught?
11. To which Italian port city do the gladiators wish to go?
12. Who are Isis and Serapis?

INTERMISSION

13. During his report to the Senate, we learn that Glabrus, the commander of the Roman garrison, was supposed to have surrounded his camp with something. What was it?
14. What traditional Roman penalty is imposed upon Glabrus for his failure?
15. What is the reason why the senators cannot simply allow the slaves to leave Italy?
16. Where are Metapontum and Brundisium? Where is Capua located relative to these cities?
17. What is a *lanista*? [**HINT**: we hear this term used when the arrival of Lentulus Batiatus is announced to Crassus.]
18. Describe the standards which are carried by the Roman soldiers. What are the letters which appear on them?
19. How are Crassus' troops arrayed before the battle with Spartacus?
20. Whose armies are said to be joining with Crassus for the battle with Spartacus?
21. What was the outcome of Crassus' battle with Spartacus?
22. What penalty do the Romans inflict upon the captured slaves? Where is this done?
23. How many slaves were punished in this way?
24. How did Spartacus die?

Answer the following questions when the film is over:
1. Look up the answers to the second parts of questions 3 and 9 above.
2. Describe the equipment used to train the gladiators in the gladiatorial school.
3. Is the "Gracchus" mentioned in this movie supposed to be one of the famous agrarian reformers, Tiberius and Gaius Gracchus? Why would this be historically impossible?
4. Which factors combined to induce Spartacus to rebellion?
5. In the film, Glabrus is said to have taken six cohorts with him against Spartacus. If these had been *full cohorts*, how many men would have been involved?

Sample Quiz and Examination Questions For *Spartacus*

Short Answer

Using our class discussions and your reading from Plutarch as sources of information, list five details or episodes from the film *Spartacus* which were *not* historical. Why might the author of the screenplay have changed these elements of the plot when creating the film?

Essay

The name *Spartacists* or *Spartacusbund* was used by a radical faction of the Social Democratic Party in Germany during World War I. The Spartacists were angered by the support for that war among other socialist groups and hoped to create an international uprising of workers. This uprising, the Spartacists believed, might force an end to the war and destroy capitalism in the process. Based upon what you have learned during this unit, why might the Spartacists have named themselves after Spartacus? What did Spartacus come to symbolize to later people? What did Spartacus represent to the ancient Romans themselves? How might citizens in a democratic state see Spartacus as representing their ideals? How might citizens in a communist state see Spartacus as representing *their* ideals?   [50 points]

Take Home Essay

Howard Fast, in the preface to his novel *Spartacus* [New York, NY: Crown Publishers, 1958], says the following about the tale which he will tell: "It is a story of brave men and women who lived long ago, and whose names have never been forgotten. The heroes of this story cherished freedom and human dignity, and lived nobly and well." The novel also ends with these words: "A time would come when Rome would be torn down -- not by slaves alone, but by slaves and serfs and peasants and by free barbarians who joined with them. And so long as men labored, and other men took and used the fruit of those who labored, the name of Spartacus would be remembered, whispered sometimes and shouted loud and clear at other times." Based upon your reading of these passages, what did Spartacus come to symbolize for Howard Fast? What did Rome come to symbolize for him? In light of what you know about Spartacus and about Rome, do these views seem to be justified? Why or why not?